Traditional Japanese Reiki Seminars

Reiki Pure and Simple

Volume IV

The Teacher Manual

By Anny J. Slegten

Reiki Pure and Simple
Volume IV: The Teacher Manual

Anny Slegten
Published by
Kimberlite Publishing House
www.kimberlitePublishingHouse.com

©2022 by Anny Slegten   01152022
All Rights Reserved. Printed in the United States.

No part of this book may be reproduced, stored in or introduced into a retrieval system, or transmitted, in any form or by any means – electronic, mechanical, photocopying, recording or otherwise – without the prior written permission of the copyright owner.

The author of this book does not dispense medical advice or prescribe the use of any technique as a form of treatment for physical, emotional, mental, spiritual or medical problems without the advice of a physician, either directly or indirectly. The intent of the author is only to offer information of a general nature to help you in your quest for physical, mental, emotional and spiritual wellbeing.

In the event you use any of the information in this book for yourself, which is your right, the author and the publisher assume no responsibility for your actions.

ISBN: 978-1-7775332-1-2
School logo designed by Anny Slegten
Book layout by Colin Christopher www.colinchristopher.com
Book cover and Kimberlite Logo designed by
Marietta Miller
http://www.execugraphx.com

The Kimberlite-Diamond Connection

Kimberlite is a rock type that was first categorized over a 100 years ago based on descriptions of the diamond-bearing pipes of Kimberley, South Africa.

Kimberlites are the mechanism by which diamonds are brought to the surface.

Kimberlitic rocks are the most important primary source of diamonds and the main rock type in which significant diamond deposits have been found so far.

Anny is familiar with many rocks and minerals as her husband was raised around quarries, and later worked in several mines in Canada.

Therefore, it was natural for Anny to choose kimberlite as an analogy to the soul residing within our body – as a diamond within the kimberlite.

Dedication

With profound gratitude, I am dedicating this book to Mikao Usui who developed such a simple and effective way to make us understand the power of our focus and our intent.

In this life, having lived on three continents and observing many ethnic cultural backgrounds, the reality of life is that whoever or wherever we are, there are no "ifs" nor "buts".

The power is truly within us – that we like it or not.

With Love and Light,

Anny Slegten

The original Usui Reiki is pure and simple. Let us keep it that way.

The reason?

"The simpler the understanding, the more powerful the result"

- unknown

Introduction

Born in Belgium in a beautiful city situated in the Flanders' Fields where the poppies grow, I was raised in a country now called La République Démocratique du Congo from 18 months old until coming to Canada at age 25. This was not a pleasant experience since I lost my country and left everything and everyone I cherished behind.

During the Independence upheaval, Immigration Officers were there, trying to entice us to move in the country they were representing.

We spoke French, and the Canadian Immigration Officer won us, explaining Canada is a bilingual country, speaking French and English – from coast to coast to coast. Well, although it is true now, it was not so at the time. When we came to Canada, we quickly learned to speak English!

Experiencing life in three continents with many different nationalities, cultures, and religions, I developed a way of thinking sometimes not well understood.

English is the fifth language I learned to speak – the reason my way of explaining myself may not always feel right to you – my dear readers.

What I write has been cautiously edited to keep my identity. Should you read some of my other books, hear me in a presentation, talk to me, have a private session with me, or take one of my courses: I want to make sure you know I am the one who wrote the book.

Thank you for reading me.

With gratitude,

Anny

Reiki Pure And Simple Volume IV:

The Teacher Manual

By Anny Slegten

LEVEL 4 TEACHER'S CHECKLIST

ROOM SET UP

[ ] Chairs - in a circle
[ ] Table(s), linen, and pillows - for "tablework" & workshop supplies
[ ] Recorded music
[ ] Clock - to pace yourself
[ ] Flowers etc.
[ ] Tea/coffee/water, etc.
[ ] Potato chips - for grounding
[ ] Student's class material
[ ] Address books, receipts, pens
[ ] Student's names, the way they want it on their certificates
[ ] Certificates, ready to be printed
[ ] Teacher's Aids
[ ] Wig stand
[ ] Initiation music you will play
[ ] Recorded music for "tablework" and meditations
[ ] Teddy bears for distant healing practice

_____
_____
_____
_____
_____
_____
_____
_____

TABLE OF CONTENTS

Dedication	vii
Level 4 Teachers Checklist	xii
Introduction	ix
Level 4 Content Color Coded	xiv
Getting Started	15
Reiki Level One	31
Reiki Level Two	73
Reiki Level Three	89
Reiki Level Four	107-3
General Information	109
Online Store, Contact, and More	119
Other books by Anny Slegten	121
Your Personal Notes	129
Who is Anny Slegten?	139

LEVEL 4 CONTENT COLOUR CODED

Teachers Checklist

Class Agenda

Japanese Writing

Attunements

The Healing Attunement

Meditation On The Symbols

Teachers Supplies

Traditional Japanese Reiki Seminars

This book belongs to

Name _____

Mailing Address _____

_____

City or Town _____

Province _____ Postal Code _____

Telephone   Home ( ) _____   Work ( ) _____

Seminar Location _____

Seminar Dates   First Degree _____

Second Degree _____

Third Degree _____

Master/Teacher _____

Anny Slegten   **Your Reiki Master/Teacher:**

The Reiki Training Centre of Canada   Name: _____
P.O. Box 3294
Sherwood Park, Alberta, T8H 2T2   Certification Number: _____
Canada

Telephone 780.448.0817
Canada 1.800.330.5999
Facsimile 780.922.1147

TRADITIONAL JAPANESE REIKI WORKSHOPS

Traditional Japanese Reiki is taught in four levels:

First Degree (or Level I)
The practitioner will be trained to give "hands-on" sessions to others as well as to themselves. In Japan, this training is given in one day, and includes four attunements to increase the flow of energy through the practitioner's hands. To accommodate our Western minds, we give the First Degree in one evening and one day. Reiki history, the practitioner's lineage, and the philosophy behind the system are also taught.

Second Degree (or Level II)
The practitioner learns how to enhance the energy transfer by increasing their focus by means of three Usui Reiki "symbols" as well as do "Distance Healing" for individuals, groups, and circumstances. During this one-day workshop, the Practitioner receives three additional attunement. As in Japan, we recommended the Practitioner take the First Degree and the Second Degree in one weekend. The true philosophy of Reiki is as gentle and simple as it is powerful and is comfortable to learn in one weekend. Any First Degree Reiki Practitioner may attend this class. When taking Second Degree Reiki only, the Student is required to attend the full weekend workshop. Proof of First Degree Reiki will be required.

Third Degree (or Level III)
In this workshop, the practitioner is attuned to and receives the fourth Usui Symbol referred to as "The Master Symbol". This symbol is the master of the four Usui Symbols, unlocking all doors so to speak, in the same context as a master key opens all locks. In Japan, this workshop is given in one day, and one has to review First Degree and Second Degree to be eligible for the Third Degree workshop. Therefore, we give the Third Degree workshop the day following the First Degree and Second Degree workshop so the Practitioner fulfills the reviewing requirements directly prior to attending the Third Degree. The Third Degree is a profound experience and may be taken when the Second Degree Reiki Students feel ready to continue their training. Second Degree Reiki Practitioner as well as Reiki Masters of any Reiki lineage may attend this workshop. Proof of Practitioner's level of Reiki will be required as well as attendance to the full workshop.

Master/Teacher Traditional Japanese Reiki Training
In Japan, a Teacher is referred to as a Master. This practical and "hands-on" workshop starts with learning to give attunements and then learning to conduct Traditional Japanese Reiki classes by assisting in a First, Second, and Third Degree Traditional Japanese Reiki workshop. Information on Reiki as taught and practised in North America and on Tibetan Reiki will be given, as well as information on the Reiki Alliance and other Reiki organizations. After completing this workshop, the Reiki Masters are qualified and able to conduct workshops if they so choose. Much support is available as well as reviews and updates.

In Traditional Japanese Reiki, the ratio is one Reiki Master for a maximum of four students. Occasionally pooling their resources, Japanese organize classes of up to 60 students with up to 20 Reiki Masters/Teachers. This requires consistency in the way Traditional Japanese Reiki is taught.

Reiki Pure and Simple Volume IV: The Teacher Manual   19

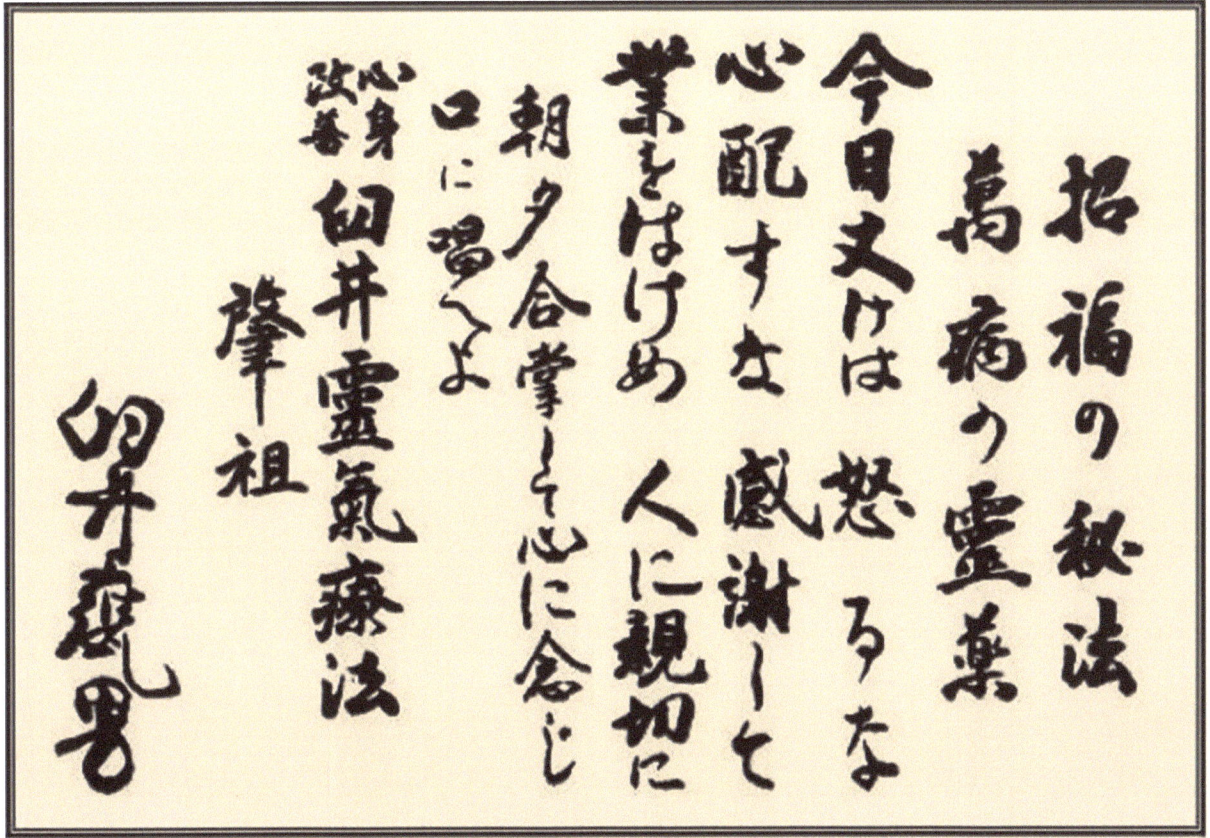

Reiki Precepts

Everything being "orally reported", it is not sure where the Reiki Precepts are coming from.
All what is known is that Mikao Usui suggested meditating on the Five Precepts
According to a legend, this was suggested by the Meiji Emperor. Another explanation of the origin is found on the following page.
This photocopy shows the Precepts in old Kanji, written 2 years after Mikao Usui's death
by Juzaburo Ushida, 2nd president of Usui Reiki Ryako Gakkai

臼井霊気療法「教義」の原点（典拠）

大正3年（1914）12月28日発行の鈴木美山博士の著書「健全の原理」という書籍の巻頭に載っている「健全の道」という題の付いた以下の文言に基づき、臼井先生が創作されたと言われています。

「　今日だけは

　　　怒らず、恐れず、正直に、

　　　　　職務に励み、人に親切に　」　　美山

The Source of Usui Reiki Ryoho Principles (Five Precepts)

It is believed that Usui Sensei created so-called Five Principles or Five Precepts based on the phrase in the opening page of a book "Kenzen-no-genri" or "the Principle of Soundness" written by Dr. Suzuki Bizan, and published on December 28, in the 3rd year of Taisho (1914).

The PHRASE titled "A Path to Soundness" reads:
[Today only
    Be not angry,
        Be not fearful,
            With honesty,
                Perform diligently your duty,
                    Be kind to others.]
                          By Bizan

KOMYO REIKI KAI
光明レイキ會

From Reverend Hyakuten Inamoto, Reiki Teacher
www.komyo-reiki.com

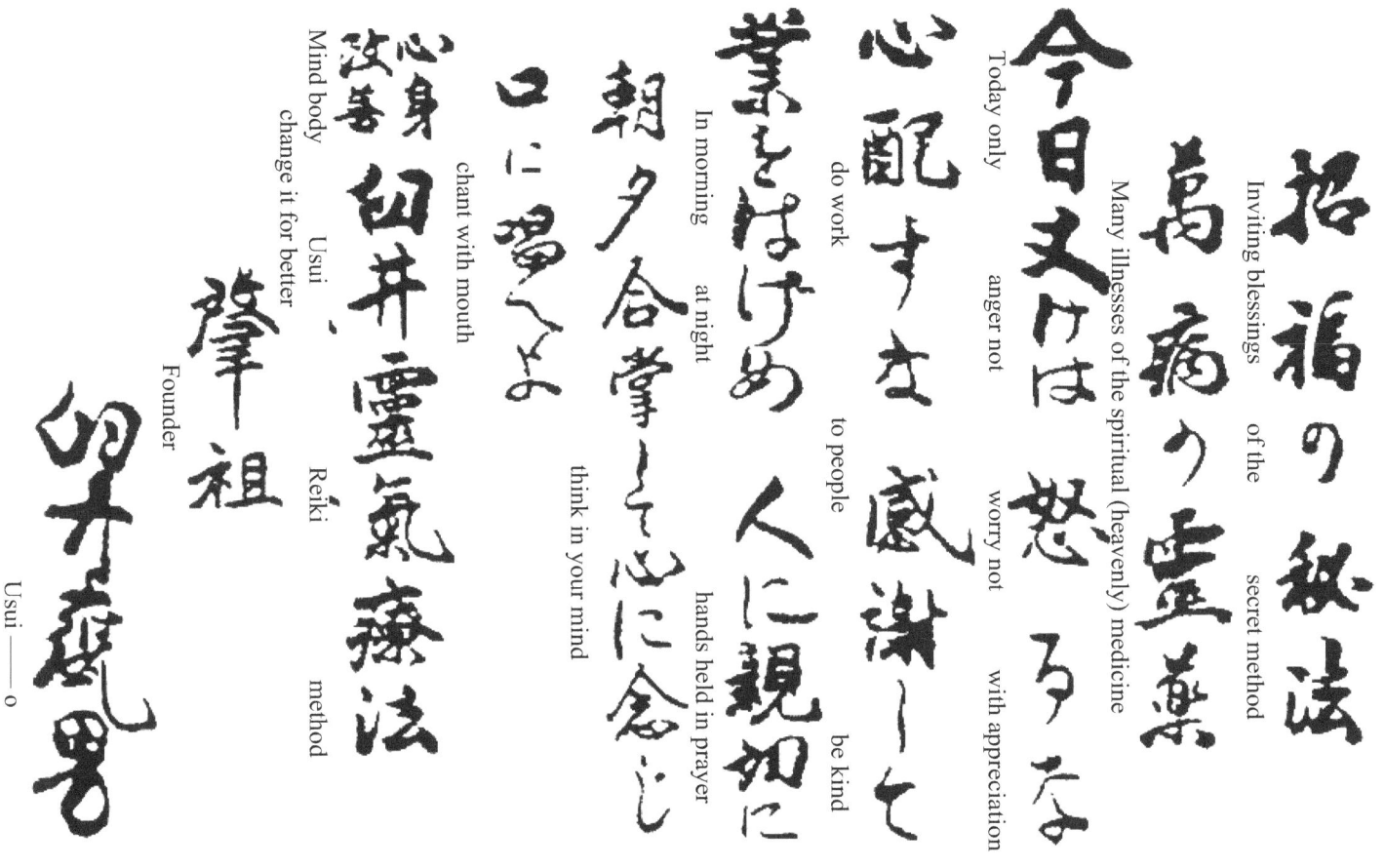

(Literal Translation)

Inviting blessings of the secret method

Many illnesses of the spiritual (heavenly) medicine

Today only anger not, worry not, with appreciation do work, to people be kind

in morning, at night, hands held in prayer think in your mind chant with mouth

Mind body changer for better Usui Reiki method

Founder Usui (Mikao)

Note that the structure is the same as in French (i.e. the verb comes first).

Usui Precepts

(In modern English)

The Secret Method of Inviting Blessings
The Spiritual Medicine of Many Illnesses

For today only, do not anger, do not worry.
Do your work with appreciation.
Be kind to all people.

In the morning and at night,
with hands held in prayer,
think this in your mind,
chant this with your mouth.

The Usui Reiki method
to change your mind and body for the better.

The founder (Mikao) Usui

The English translation was put on the Internet August 24, 1996 by Rick Rivard, a slightly non-traditional Reiki Master living in Vancouver, British Columbia Canada.

It was translated by Emiko Arai a Japanese living in Canada for some time now, a group of Reiki Masters which included Dave King, and with the help of a very good Japanese to English dictionary.

Anny's Spiritual Lineage

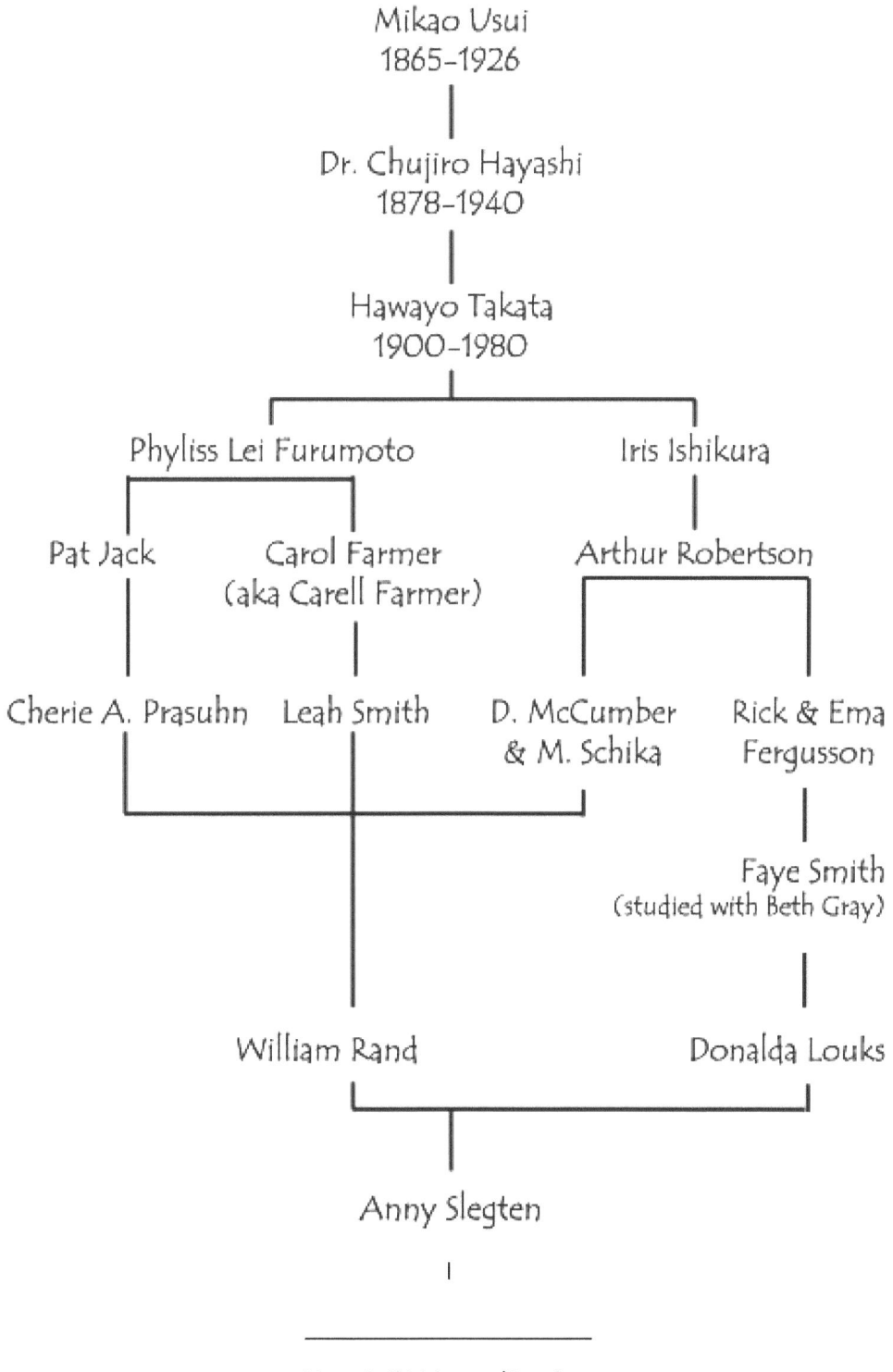

Lineage

Anny Slegten's *"Japanese Connections"*

Mikao Usui was born in 1865. During his time in Tokyo, there were many forms of healing hands, and Usui's method was the easiest to learn and use. According to chronicles of the time, Usui was a very popular healer, and considered a pioneer in this area of healing. He went to Tokyo where he opened his school in 1921. He passed away in 1926.

Books: "Healing Hands", by Reiki Master Toshitaka Mochizuki,
and an older book by Takichi Tsukida, "The Secret of How to Take Care of Your Family Members".

There are four known students of Usui's.

1923   Toshihiro Eguchi was already a very strong healer when he learned Reiki. One of Eguchi's students was Goro Miyazuki.

1925   Dr. Hayashi took the training at 47 years of age.

At the same time, two other naval officers took the training, Jusaburo Giuda and Bo Taketomi. Reiki Master Toshitaka Mochizuki has connections to many Reiki Masters in Japan, some who have a lineage going back to Toshihiro Iguchi. A group of 10 of these masters, including Toshitaka Mochizuki, hold monthly Reiki training classes for up to 40 students at a time. Toshitaka Mochizuki opened a Reiki school in 1994 where over 700 people have attended Reiki classes so far.

One of Anny Slegten's students, David King, went to Japan in November 1995, and in April 1996. Having attended Reiki classes and experienced attunements many times, David King brought back information on Reiki as it was practiced in Japan. Anny Slegten is grateful to David for being instrumental in her receiving information about Reiki from the source, and being put in contact with Toshitaka Mochizuki.

In Japan, one gets their lineage through the First Degree first Reiki Teacher. In the West, we get our lineage through the Reiki Teacher who gave us the Master attunement and gave us the Teacher training. Therefore, in Japan, Anny Slegten's lineage is from Trish Dennison. In Canada, Anny's lineage includes William Rand, Toshihiro Iguchi, Goro Miyazuki, Ayumi Sato, Toshikata Mochizuki, David King.

At this time of printing this book, both Ayumi Sato and Toshitaka Mochizuki are in their 60's.

TRADITIONAL JAPANESE REIKI

The First Degree

Reiki Training Centre of Canada   Anny Slegten, P.O. Box 3294, Sherwood Park, Alberta, Canada T8H 2T2
Telephone 780.448.0817 Toll Free 1.800.330.5999 Facsimile 780.922.1147 www.reiki-canada.com

Traditional Japanese Reiki **First Degree Workshop**

Evening

[ ] Registration, Names (for certificates) address & telephone numbers

[ ] Explain routine/starting time/intermissions/lunch etc.

[ ] **Self introduction to the group, your own story:**
   Remember, you are setting the tone for the whole workshop

_____

_____

[ ] Group introduction:

      [ ] First name

      [ ] What do you know about Reiki

      [ ] Their reason to take the workshop

[ ] Reiki background
[ ] Personal experiences about the purpose and results of attunements
[ ] Explain attunement procedure and demonstrate positions used (same 4 X)

_____

_____

[ ] **First attunement** »»> make them ask for a gift
              »»> make them practice hand positions on self
[ ] Feedback »»> "write down your experience"
[ ] Energy "brush down"
[ ] Homework: Hold hands 3 to minute
on yes - Heart Chakra - Solar Plexus

[ ] Tomorrow's agenda:
    starting time - Lunch - Estimated finishing time

Next Morning

[ ] Welcome back
[ ] Feedback on homework
[ ] Demonstrate hand positions for self

[ ] **Second attunement**

»» make them ask for a gift
»»> make them practice hand positions on self

[ ] Feedback »»> "write down your experience"
[ ] More talk on Reiki

[ ] **Third attunement**

»»> make them ask for a gift
»»> make them practice hand positions on self

[ ] Feedback »»> "write down your experience"

Set up table during lunch hour

[ ] **Demonstrate hand position for client**
[ ] Group "tablework" »»> unbalanced
»»> balanced
[ ] Feedback »»> written or verbal, use your own judgement
[ ] Demonstrat.e a quick chair session
[ ] Students practice chair session

[ ] **Fourth attunement** »»> make them ask for a gift
»»> make them practice hand positions on self
[ ] Feedback »»> "write down your experience"
[ ] Do distant healing by holding a picture between the palm of hands
[ ] Homework: Hold hands 3 to 5 minutes on
     Eyes - Heart Chakra - and where your hands want to go
[ ] Tomorrow's agenda for 2nd degree Reiki
     Starting time - Lunch - Estimated finishing time
[ ] Bring a Teddy Bear for distant healing practice

[ ] **Distribute certificates**

FIRST DEGREE ATTUNEMENTS Four identical attunements

Perform procedure

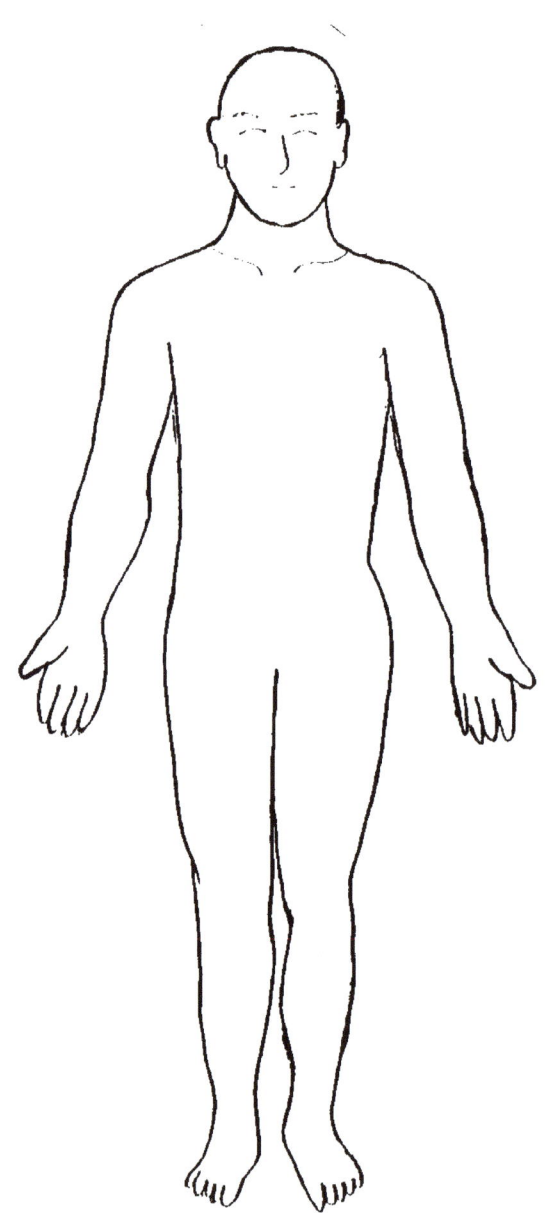

FIRST DEGREE ATTUNEMENTS Four identical attunements

Perform procedure

FIRST DEGREE ATTUNEMENTS Four identical attunements.

1- Review hand position on self and suggest the students to Reiki themselves after the attunement,

When having left the room, waiting for all the other students to be attuned, the student may Reiki themselves or someone else sitting in the room.

2- Demonstrate on yourself the hand positions during the attunement, and request they put their hands in the prayer position when they feel the Reiki Master/Teacher's hand touching the top of their head.

3- *This is what* *I learned from my first Reiki Master/Teacher:*
Suggest students to ask the Universe a gift, and signal to let you know they decided what gift they are asking for. Once every student got "it", request they now close their eyes and keep their eyes closed until you ask them to open them.

4- Standing behind the student and draw the Master Symbol in the air and move it over your own body.

  - BOW, as to say hello.

  - Clear the student's energy field by making three descending sweeps of the hand from above the student's head to the ground.

  - Place on hand on (or just above) the student's crown chakra and your other hand just above your first hand. **Perform procedure.**

  - Place your hands on the student's shoulders and **perform procedure.**

- Move to the left side of the student and place your left hand on the student's forehead and your right hand on the student's occiput and **perform procedure.**

- Sit/kneel/stand in front of the student and place your hands on the student's ankles, just below the ankle bone, and **perform procedure.**

- Sit/kneel/stand in front of the student and place your hands over the student's hands held in prayer and **perform procedure**.

- Sit/kneel/stand in front of the student and open/separate the student's hands.

- Place each of your hands slightly above the student's hands and **perform procedure**.

- Place each of your hands slightly below the student's hands and **perform procedure**.

- Place one hand slightly above the student's right hand and your other hand slightly below the student's right hand and **perform procedure**.

- Place one hand slightly above the student's left hand and your other hand slightly below the student's left hand and **perform procedure**.

- Stand in front of the student and place the student's hands back into the prayers position and blow gently and continuously along the space between the hands, going from the thumb side palm to the little finger side palm **with the intention of sealing the initiation into the palm of the hands**. Rotate the student's hands while doing so.

- Still holding the student's hands, give a short, sharp blast of breath to the student's crown chakra, heart chakra and the dantien chakra (just below the navel).

- *This is my idea*: Still holding the student's hands, I silently wish them "to heal, clear, resolve and dissolve, whatever has to be healed, cleared resolved and dissolved".

- Go behind the student and make a single upward sweep of the hand, from the floor to above the student's head, (as to close the door).

- Bow, as to say 'goodbye'.

- Take the student's right hand and place it on the student's left shoulder.

- Take the student's left hand and place it on the student's right shoulder.

- Place your hands on the student's shoulders and give them a gentle tug.

5- When the initiations are completed, ask the student(s) to open their eyes stay silent and in the privacy of their own self write down their experience.

KATAKANA ALPHABET

ア	カ	サ	タ	ナ	ハ	マ	ヤ	ラ	ワ
イ	キ	シ	チ	ニ	ヒ	ミ	主	リ	ン
ウ	ク	ス	ツ	ヌ	フ	ム	ユ	ル	
エ	ケ	セ	テ	ネ	ヘ	メ	エ	レ	
オ	コ	ソ	ト	ノ	ホ	モ	ヨ	ロ	

a	ka	sa	ta	na	ha	ma	ya	ra	wa
i	ki	shi	chi	ni	hi	mi	(yi)	ri	n/m
u	ku	su	tsu	nu	fu	mu	yu	ru	
e	ke	se	te	ne	he	me	(ye)	re	
o	ko	so	to	no	ho	mo	yo	ro	

WRITING AND PRONUNCIATION

There are three kinds of Japanese writing:
1. *Kanji:* Chinese characters or ideographs, each conveying an idea, most of which have at least two readings.
2. *Hiragana:* A phonetic syllabary. The symbols are curvilinear in style.
1. *Katakana:* The second syllabary used primarily for foreign names and place names and words of foreign origin. The symbols are made up of straight lines.

Written Japanese normally makes use of all three, as in the following example:

"I am going to Canada." 私はカナダに行きます。

kanji	**Watashi** 私		**i-** 行
hiragana	**wa** は	**ni** に	**kimasu** きます
katakana		**Kanada** カナダ	

Besides these three forms of writing, Japanese is sometimes written in *romaji* (Roman letters), particularly for the convenience of foreigners. This is generally used in teaching conversational Japanese to foreigners when time is limited. There are various systems for transliterating Japanese in the Roman alphabet. In this book we use the modified Hepburn system.

HIRAGANA, KATAKANA AND RŌMAJI

The *kana* to the left are *hiragana*; *katakana* are in parentheses.

I Basic Syllables: Vowel, Consonant plus vowel and **n**

c \ v	a	i	u	e	o
	a あ (ア)	i い (イ)	u う (ウ)	e え (エ)	o お (オ)
k	ka か (カ)	ki き (キ)	ku く (ク)	ke け (ケ)	ko こ (コ)
s	sa さ (サ)	shi し (シ)	su す (ス)	se せ (セ)	so そ (ソ)
t	ta た (タ)	chi ち (チ)	tsu つ (ツ)	te て (テ)	to と (ト)
n	na な (ナ)	ni に (ニ)	nu ぬ (ヌ)	ne ね (ネ)	no の (ノ)
h	ha は (ハ)	hi ひ (ヒ)	fu ふ (フ)	he へ (ヘ)	ho ほ (ホ)
m	ma ま (マ)	mi み (ミ)	mu む (ム)	me め (メ)	mo も (モ)
y	ya や (ヤ)	[i い (イ)]	yu ゆ (ユ)	[e え (エ)]	yo よ (ヨ)
r	ra ら (ラ)	ri り (リ)	ru る (ル)	re れ (レ)	ro ろ (ロ)
w	wa わ (ワ)	[i い (イ)]	[u う (ウ)]	[e え (エ)]	o を (ヲ)
n, m	— ん (ン)				

Note: The syllables **yi, ye, wi, wu** and **we** do not occur in modern Japanese.

Reiki written in Japanese in different styles of Kanji writing.
Kanji means “Chinese characters”.

霊	霊 靈
気	気 氣

Katakana are characterized by short, straight strokes and sharp corners. There are two main systems of ordering katakana: the old-fashioned iroha ordering, and the more prevalent gojūon ordering.
Reiki written in Katakana, “words from somewhere else”, or “foreign sound”.

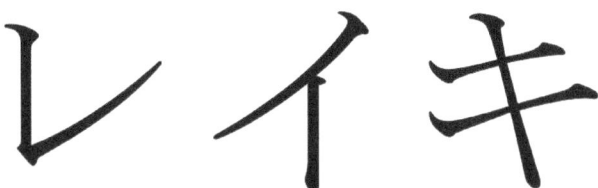

レ	イ	キ
Katakana Letter RE	Katakana Letter I	Katakana Letter KI

Reiki Training Centre of Canada Anny Slegten, P.O. Box 3294, Sherwood Park, Alberta, Canada T8H 2T2
Telephone 780.448.0817 Toll Free 1.800.330.5999 Facsimile 780.922.1147 www.reiki-canada.com

POWER
OF THE
GOD

THE PERSON
WHO SAW
THE GOD
(MIKO: secret person)

REI

Spirit
Ghost

KI

Mind
Feeling

*(Mystery you don't know,
An unacceptable mystery.)*

REIKI is pronounced "Ray - Key"

REI means "universal" and refers also to the spiritual dimension and the soul.

KI means the vital life force energy which flows through all that is alive.

The Japanese characters, when combined, present the concept of "universal life-force energy".

Reiki energy is whole, not dual. It is therefore neither positive nor negative per say, but rather is the combination of both of these qualities.

The Japanese Kanji character of Reiki as written before world War II
as drawn by Hawayo Takata in December 1979

(Kindly note: Because the original letter was photocopied so many times, it has been retyped here so that one can read it.)

I was born in Hanamaulu, Kauai, on December 24, 1900. Born of immigrant parents, I attended the public schools. I am not a college graduate, but a self-educated woman, still learning. My marriage to Saichi Takata was a happy domesticated life until sickness and death in my home and family changed the pattern of my life. I witnessed seven funerals in seven years. It was sadness and insecurity whichever way I turned. I went into deep and serious meditation, asking God to show me a way to find myself and to establish a good life for my children. I had faith to accept that there is a Supreme Being that governs the universe and all beings.

In 1935 I became very ill and entered a hospital in Tokyo. It became a reality when I was introduced to "Reiki" - the Great Universal Life Energy. The great master, Chujiro Hayashi, was the healer and the teacher of this art of healing in Tokyo. He called it the Great Life Force or Reiki in Japanese.

Since I mastered this art, I enjoy good health and have happiness and security. When I can enjoy all this, so can you and enjoy a full life, spiritually, mentally, and physically. This Life Energy serves when applied to yourself or to anything that has life, shall restore you to normal, in any devitalized condition. It cannot harm any being. It can only do good, to restore and prevent from deterioration. It can stop pain and relax your nervous tension. It takes care of acute and chronic conditions. It is a complete whole.

Now I am advancing into maturity (74), I wish to leave this noble art to all mankind who wish to have the desire to learn this art of healing, "Reiki", it helps human beings, young or old, plants, fowls, animals, fish, everything that has life. When I go into transition, it shall be left with you for you to carry on, on this earth plane. I am a simple, humble servant, serving you and God.

Thank you,

Hawayo Takata

CERTIFICATE

THIS IS TO CERTIFY that Mrs. Hawayo Takata, an American citizen born in the Territory of Hawaii, after a course of study and training in the Usui system of Reiki healing undertaken under my personal supervision during a visit to Japan in 1935 and subsequently, has passed all the tests and proved worthy and capable of administering the treatment and of conferring the power of Reiki on others.

THEREFORE I, Dr. Chujiro Hayashi, by virtue of my authority as a Master of the Usui Reiki system of drugless healing, do hereby confer upon Mrs. Hawayo Takata the full power and authority to practice the Reiki system and to impart to others the secret knowledge and the gift of healing under this system.

MRS. HAWAYO TAKATA is hereby certified by me as a practitioner and Master of Dr. Usui's Reiki system of healing, at this time the only person in the United States authorized to confer similar powers on others and one of the thirteen fully qualified as a Master of the profession.

Signed by me this 21st day of February, 1938, in the city and county of Honolulu, territory of Hawaii.

Witness to his signature:

(SIGNED) *Chujiro Hayashi*

TERRITORY OF HAWAII. } ss.
City and County of Honolulu.

On this 21st day of February A. D. 1938, before me personally appeared
• • • • • • • • • • (DR.) CHUJIRO HAYASHI • • • • • • • • • • • • • • •
to me known to be the person described in and who executed the foregoing instrument and acknowledged that WHO executed the same as HIS free act and deed.

Notary Public, First Judicial Circuit,
Territory of Hawaii.

Reiki Certificate Awarded to Hawayo Takata in 1938

Dr. Chujiro Hayashi
(1878-1940)

Mrs Hawayo Takata
(1900-1980)

Mikao Usui
(1865-1926)

Mikao Usui was born in Japan. "USU" means vessel, a barrel, a container, "I" means spring water, indicating Mikao Usui's family was in the trade of collecting spring water for delivery. There are many stories about how the system came about. In my search for the real story, I found out things are very much the same here as in Japan. Some of the information is down to earth, some quite fantastic. According to some, Mikao Usui was born August 15, 1862 and died March 9, 1926. When one considers the myth that developed in less than 80 years since his death, one wonders what happened about the truth of revered religious leaders, Jesus included.

One of Mikao Usui's students was Chujiro Hayashi, a ship's doctor, who used the knowledge to open a healing clinic in Tokyo. Hayashi, whose name means forest in Japanese, developed a set of hand positions suitable for clinical use of the System, shifting the focus from using the System for oneself to using the System to heal others. At his clinic, Dr. Hayashi employed a method of healing that required several practitioners work on one client at the same time. In lieu of payment, Dr. Hayashi would request a student to work one shift a week at his clinic. It was taking a student three months to pay off his/her debt, hence the three months requirement between Levels I and II, as now recommended by the Reiki Alliance. Just like here, there are many schools of Reiki in Japan. Some schools advocate time between Levels I and II, others advocate Level I and Level II in two days. For Level II, some insist on giving one symbol at the time, several days, or weeks between the teaching of the next symbol.

As well as training his practitioners, Dr. Hayashi trained several people to teach the System. One of these was Hawayo Takata, a Japanese American from Hawaii. She had turned up at his clinic with a terminal illness which was later cured. Not expected to live and leaving her daughter at home, she had sailed from San Francisco to Yokohama to make peace with her family. At her request, Dr. Hayashi taught her the system and Hawayo Takata was made a Master/Teacher on February 21, 1938 (a copy of the notarized certificate can be found on page 3). During the war that followed, Dr. Hayashi's clinic was bombed (May 10, 194?). Dr. Hayashi was never to be found, and it is believed he was at his clinic when it was destroyed.

I am most grateful to Hawayo Takata and her successors to have spread the system throughout North America and parts of Europe. In Japan, just like here, many claim of teaching Reiki in its original form. Although it has been modified with time, the Usui System of Natural Healing known as Reiki is so powerful that it works, no matter how one paints it.

May I suggest you read as many books as possible on the subject, including Reiki Fire by Frank Arjava Petter, a Reiki Master and Teacher having lived in Japan for about 12 years, experience Reiki, and make up your own mind on the matter. May you understand the principle behind the system and remember: the beauty of the Usui System of Natural Healing known to us as Reiki lies in its simplicity. Let us keep it that way.

The Energy "Brush Down"

This was originally taught by Mikao Usui to clear one's energy field and is to be practiced before and sometimes after a session.

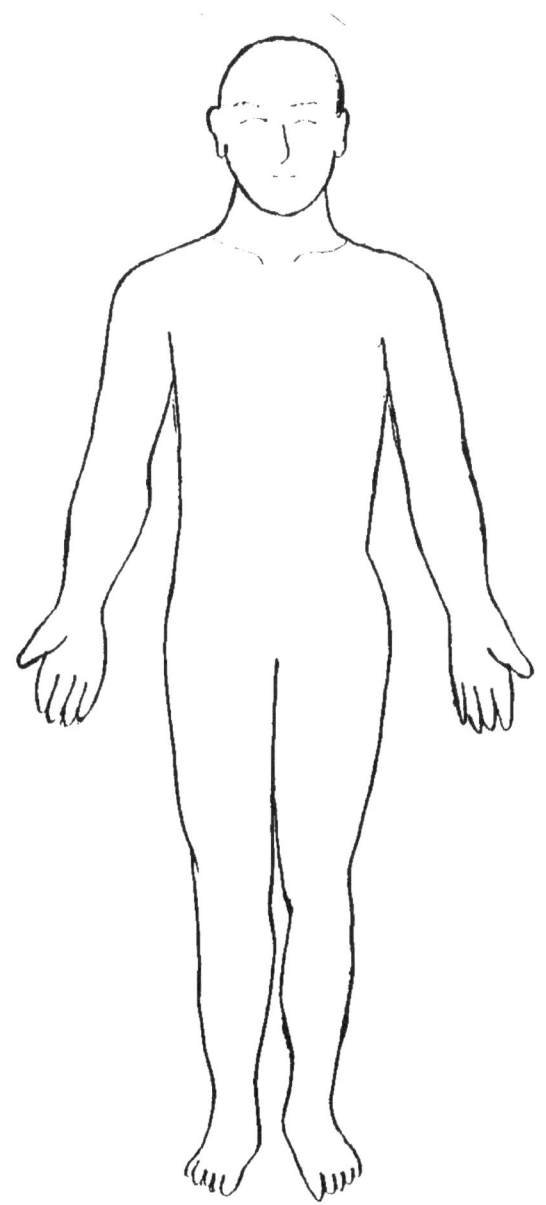

Left hand on right shoulder to left hip.

Right hand on left shoulder to right hip.

Left hand to back of right arm from shoulder to back of hand.

Right hand to back of left arm from shoulder to back of hand.

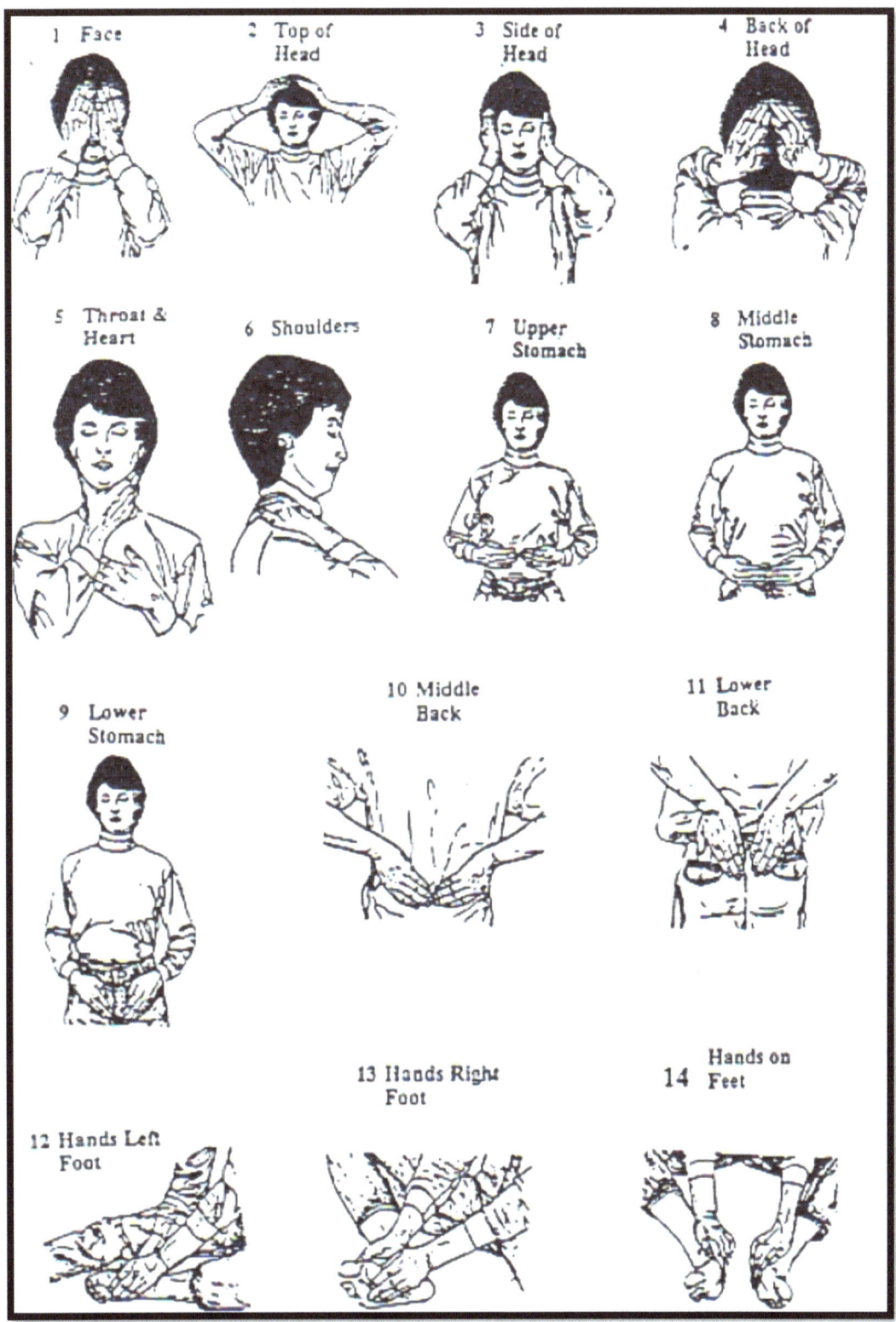

Hand Positions for Self-Treatment

From William Rand

Reiki Pure and Simple Volume IV: The Teacher Manual

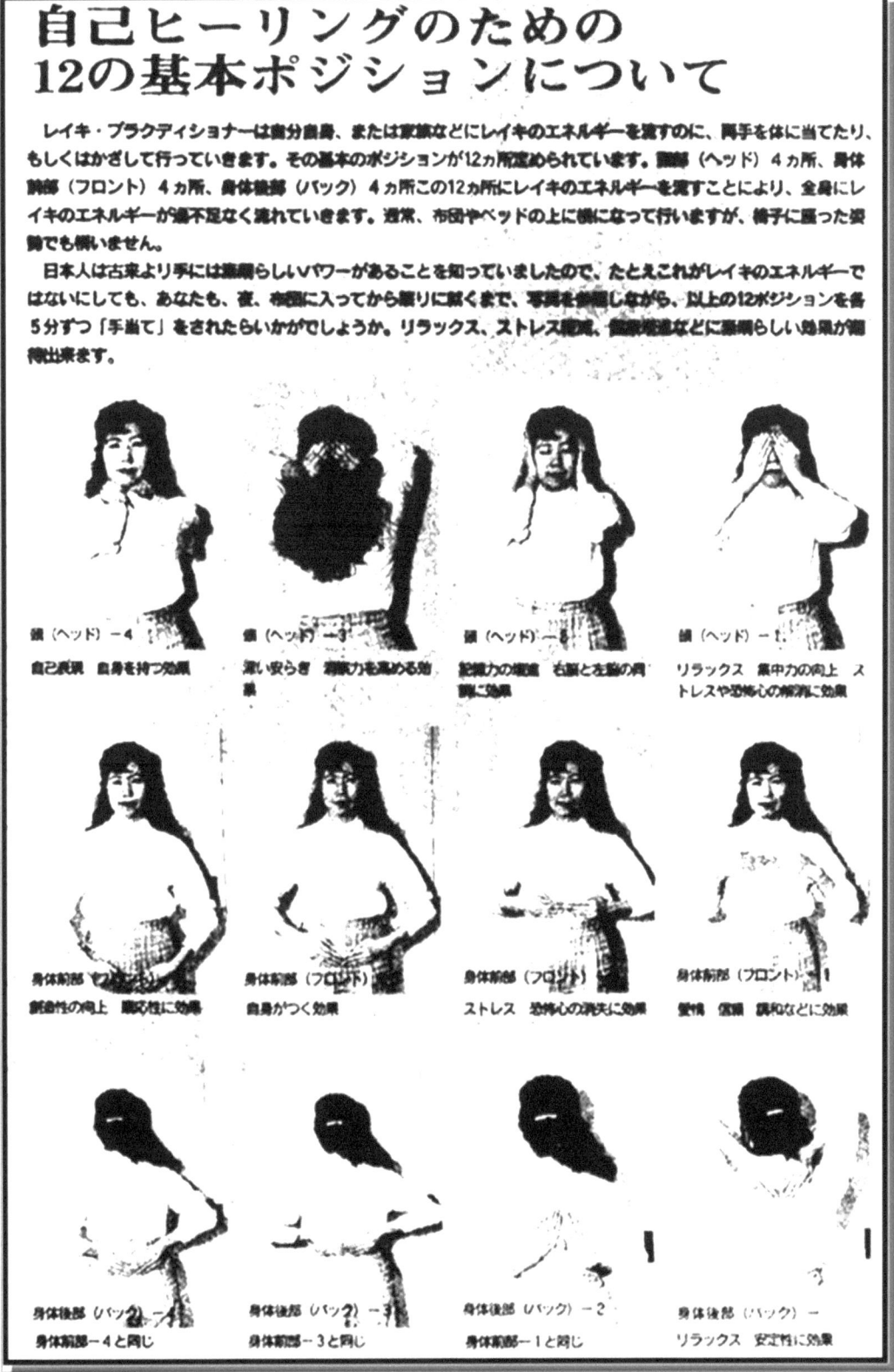

Advertising enclosed with Toshikata Mochizuki's book on Reiki ordered by mail.

Major Chakras

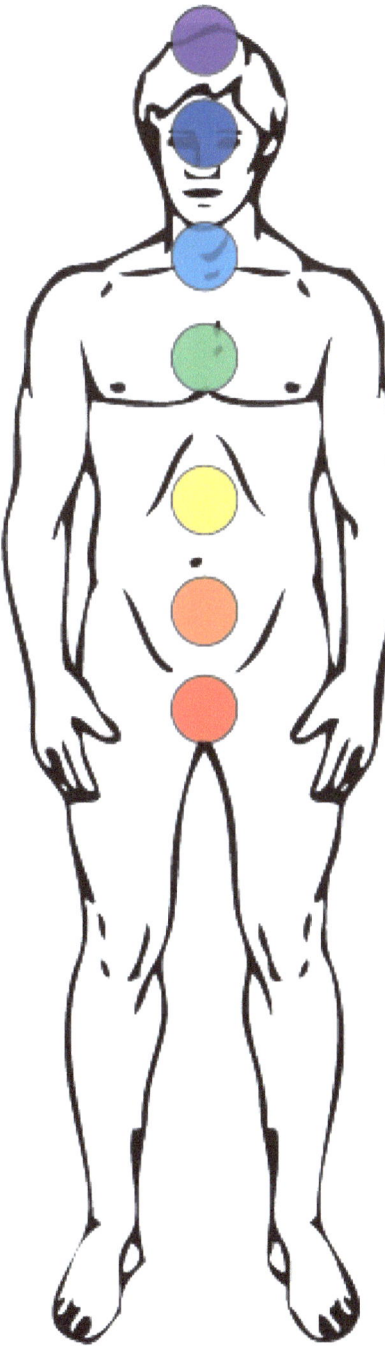

Crown - Violet — Spiritual Awareness

Brow - Indigo — Intuition, Intellect

Throat - Blue — Communication, Self-expression

Heart - Green — Unconditional Love, Compassion

Solar Plexus - Yellow — Power, Creativity, Emotions

Base - Orange — Sexuality, Relationships, Emotions

Root - Red — Survival, Procreation

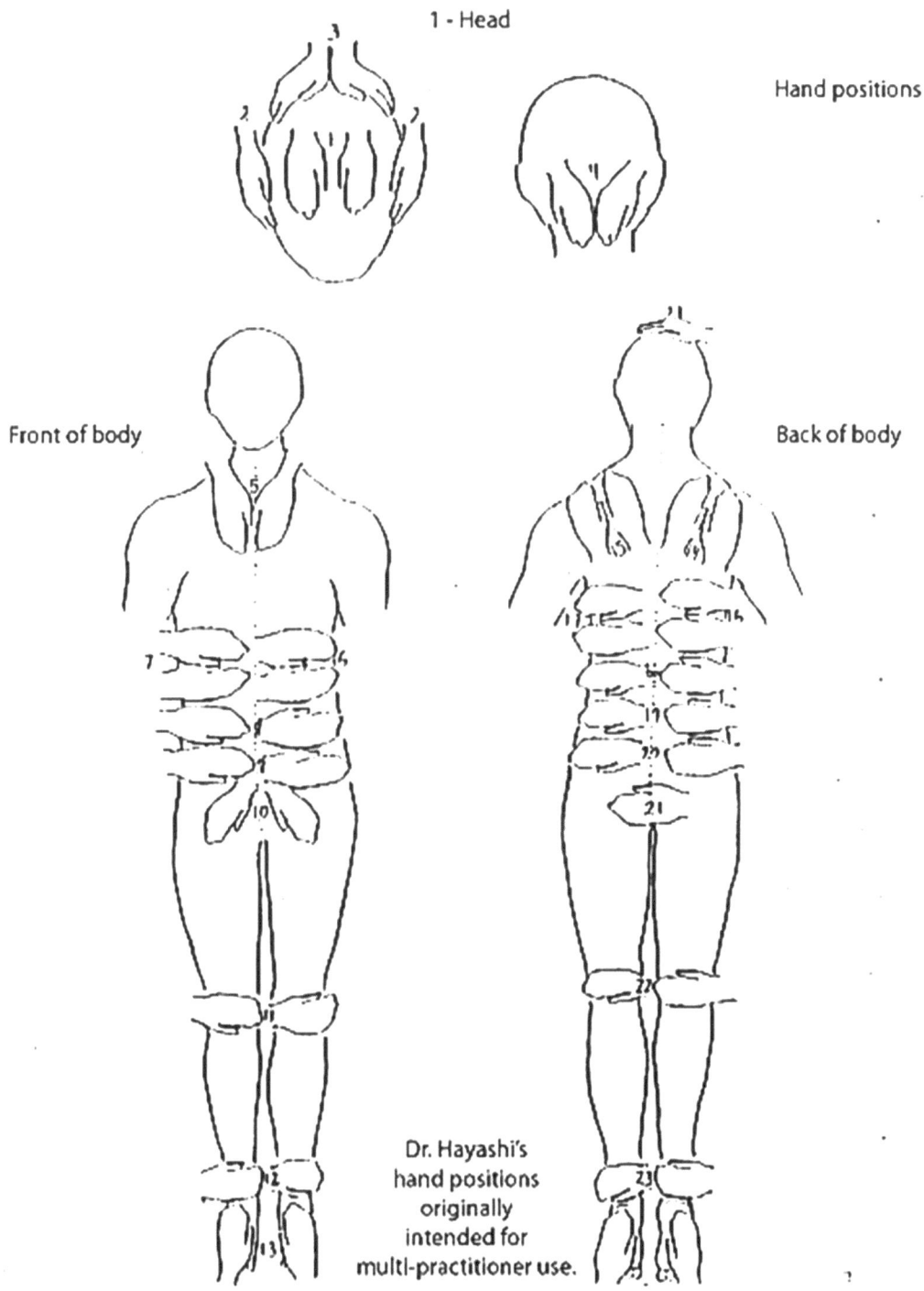

Reiki Positions
Head and full body positions:

Please note:
It is believed these instructions are Dr. Hayashi's hand positions intended for use in his medical clinic.

1. **Over forehead**, eyes and cheeks (cover eyes with tissue). Treats cataracts, glaucoma, sinuses, allergies, asthma, nerves, and brain. Pituitary is the gland which affects all other glands of the body, i.e. thymus, thyroid, ovaries, adrenals, pancreas, liver, prostate. Sixth chakra - 3rd eye - stress, confusion.

2. **Over temples** - balances right (intuition/wisdom) and left (rational/logical/sequential) hemispheres of the brain. Over ears treats eyes, ears (contact for spinal nerves, heart, gall bladder, liver, kidneys, colon, abdomen, lungs, stomach, muscles, veins, brain, amnesia).

3. **Across top of head** - treats pressure headaches, eye pain, abdominal cramps, gas, indigestion, multiple sclerosis. Back of head - balances energy between pituitary and pineal glands, treats brain, colon, enlarged legs, bloat, excess fluid, stress and emotions.

4. **Over back of head** - fingers under occipital ridge treats eyes, sight, headaches, nose bleeding, hay fever, sinuses, stroke, spleen, indigestion, stroke, sorrow, relaxes and clears thoughts. Medulla oblongata has connection to the third eye.

Optional positions - sides and front of neck, thyroid (important for metabolism, malfunctioning thyroid can cause heart palpitation, loss of weight, excessive weight), also involved in body temperature control, high and low blood pressure (veins in side of neck), treats flu, colds, tonsils, whiplash. Fifth chakra, resentment, frustration, communication, self-expression.

5. **Over heart and thymus gland** - treats lungs, heart problems, bronchitis, lymph (immune system), deafness. Emotions - depression, hate, fourth chakra.

6. **Left of Diaphragm** - over part of the stomach, pancreas, spleen, intestines, colon. Treats anemia, leukemia, diabetes, digestion, immune system.

7. Right of Diaphragm - over liver, gall bladder, part of stomach, pancreas, duodenum and intestines. Treats hepatitis, gall stones, hypoglycemia, diabetes, liver (very important organ for detoxification), resentment, depression.

8 / 9. **Over navel and solar plexus**, stomach; intestines, colon, heart, digestion, lymph, shock - emotions, depression, fear, anger, resentment. Hara - energy center, third chakra.

10. **Hands in V position on lower abdomen** - in women - treats ovaries, fallopian tubes, uterus, vagina, bladder. In men - treats seminal ducts, urachus, bladder, also small intestine, appendix. Treats breast tumors, menopause, pregnancy, cramps, lower back pain, tumors of ovaries, vagina, cervix, bladder, seizures. Extra position over hip ball joints for varicose veins, leg pain. First chakra.

11. **Over knees** - treats circulation, flexibility, grounding.

12. **Over ankles** - treats circulation, understanding, grounding.

13. **Soles of feet** - treats circulation, grounding and all aspects of moving forward in life as well as all aspects of the physiology (e.g. reflexology).

14/15. **On shoulders** - treat for stress, breakdown, sleeplessness, anxiety, nervousness. Over 7th cervical treat for bone pain, nerves, heart, spine, bronchitis, cough.

16-18. **Over adrenals, kidneys, spleen, gall bladder, liver**. Treat for back pain, allergy, hay fever, stress, detoxification, heart problems, shock.

19/20. **Sciatic nerve, lymph, back pain, nerves**.

Optional Position - T position - treats prostate, female organs, hemorrhoids, bladder, coccyx. Indigestion, sciatic nerve, other rectal imbalances. Same as in front.

21. **Over coccyx and** 1) **top of head**, 2) **occipital notch,** 3) 7th cervical - for balancing the spine.

22. **Back of knees** - sciatic nerve.

23. **Back of ankles** - sciatic at the back of heel.

24. **Souls of feet** - completion.

SHORT TREATMENT
About 10 - 15 minutes - person seated.

1. Shoulders
2. Top of head
3. Forehead / medulla
4. Thymus, thyroid / 7th cervical
5. Heart / adrenals
6. Solar plexus / kidneys
7. Navel / back
8. Ovaries / prostate

A QUICK SESSION

Circumstances may arise where you would like to give someone a full Reiki session and cannot because there is not enough time, or you are in an area where the person cannot lie down, such as in an office. In these cases, you can still give a powerful Reiki in the form of a brief, seated session. Although it is preferable to give a complete session, a short one is better than none at all, and can bring surprising results.

Ask your client to sit comfortably in an upright chair, close their eyes, and relax.

Use your own way to center yourself.

Gently smooth your client's energy field (aura), moving in a downward motion from the top of the head. (You may wish to add in a moment of "beaming" as well, a Chinese energy technique recommended by William Rand.)

1. Gently lay your hands on your client's shoulders.
2. Lay your hands on the crown of the head (7th chakra).
3. Lay your hands on the temples.
4. Lay one hand over the forehead and eyes and the other over the base of the back of the head (6th chakra).
5. Lay one hand over the throat and the other over the back of the neck (5th chakra).
6. Lay one hand over the middle of the chest and the other over the upper back (4th chakra).
7. Lay one hand over the middle of the solar plexus and the other over the middle of the back (3rd chakra).
8. Lay one hand on the abdomen and the other on the lower back (2nd chakra).
9. Lay one hand above the groin and the other over the coccyx (1st chakra).
10. *(Optional)* While supporting your client's leg with one hand or across your lap, lay the other hand over the bottom of the feet.

You may complete the seated session by briefly smoothing up your client's aura. Ask them to breathe in deeply and slowly, and then open their eyes.

Winter 1996 Reiki News

Reiki News

Published by the Center for Reiki Training - Southfield, Michigan, U.S.A.

Advanced Reiki Techniques - Part I
by William Lee Rand

Dr. Usui provided the foundation for the practice of Reiki which was further developed by Dr. Hayashi and brought to the western world by Mrs. Takata. While a thorough understanding of the Usui system as taught by Mrs. Takata is important for a strong foundation, the serious student is often inspired to learn more.

The universe is a never-ending system of unlimited possibilities. It is always possible to improve something no matter how developed it might be. For those of us who truly want to help others, the idea of following our inner promptings to continue to develop our healing skills is something we cannot ignore.

Since Reiki makes use of life force energy for the purpose of healing, it was never meant to be a stagnant system. Like life itself, Reiki was meant to grow and develop. There are a number of techniques taught by the Center that have come from inner guidance and have proven themselves effective through experience. These techniques are not difficult to learn and make a useful addition to one's healing skills.

Scanning is a method that uses the sensitivity in the hands to determine the areas in the aura and in the physical body that are out of balance and in need of Reiki. The Reiki attunement received in Reiki I not only opens the palm chakras to channel healing energy, but also opens them to be more sensitive to the human energy field. This greater sensitivity allows one to use the hand(s) to sense the areas where Reiki is needed. This is a technique that is easily learned in the Reiki I class.

Before starting, say a short prayer asking to be shown the areas in need of Reiki. Then start by placing the non-dominate hand about 12 inches away from the client's crown chakra and sensing what the energy feels like on the surface of the palm. Once you become aware of a base line sensation in the palm, you can begin to slowly move the hand up over the face and down the body, keeping the palm about 4-6" above the body. As soon as you become aware of any change in the sensation on the surface of the palm, accept this as an indication of a distortion in the energy field and thus an area where the person needs Reiki. Once you have found an area to treat, the next step is to determine the best height above the body. Do this by moving your hand up and down slowly over the area and using your intuition. Sometimes this feels like pushing on a spring and you will often feel pressure on your hand at a certain height above the body when you reach the right height. This can be as high as several feet above the body or as low as actually touching the body or somewhere in between. Once you have found a location and the right height, bring both hands together at this spot, and begin doing Reiki. When you feel the energy flow subsiding, recheck the area with your non-dominate hand to see if it has changed and if it feels done. If so, then go on to another area.

Scanning can also be done on oneself by following the same steps. Often, when doing self-scanning, a person will become more connected to one's inner issues and achieve a greater feeling of self-love.

By scanning and treating in this way, you will be healing the human energy field thus causing it to be more unified. Then, when you do a complete treatment using all the hand positions, your Reiki energy will flow more strongly because the client's energy field is now more connected.

Reiki Training Centre of Canada   Anny Slegten, P.O. Box 3294, Sherwood Park, Alberta, Canada T8H 2T2
Telephone 780.448.0817 Toll Free 1.800.330.5999 Facsimile 780.922.1147 www.reiki-canada.com

Scanning and treating in the energy field not only treats the aura, but can also treat the physical body. Often, the energy flow will be much stronger when following this method because you will be working in an area that really needs Reiki and also because when treating out in the aura, the energy can more easily flow to many areas at once.

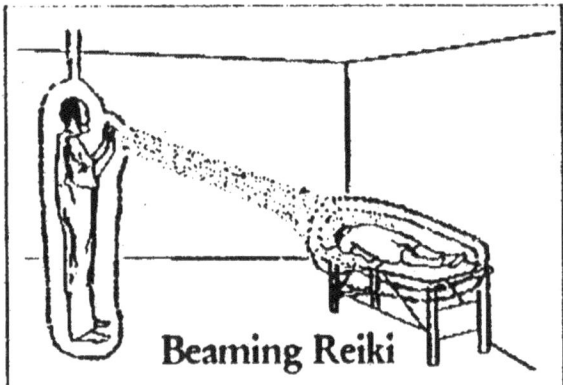

Beaming is a method of sending Reiki across the room to another person. It is taught in Reiki II and is useful for a number of reasons. First, by being outside of the client's aura, the Reiki can treat the whole person, first by treating the aura, and then by guiding itself to the areas that need Reiki the most. Because you are outside the aura, the Reiki energy has a greater surface area to work with. Also, being away from the client gives more room for one's healing guides to add their energy. I know that some will say that for the guides, space doesn't matter, but this is the information we are given from the guides. While the space taken up by physical bodies is not the issue for them, the individual's auric fields take up psychic space, so when you are further back, it gives more room for the guides to move closer and work directly with the client as well as work through you.

To do beaming, move back outside of the client's aura. Then draw out the distant symbol imagining it being drawn out in light over the client. Then bring both hands up and intend to send Reiki to the client through the palms of the hands. While beaming, hold your gaze on the person in an unfocused relaxed way intending that Reiki flow from your eyes as well as your hands. Allow yourself to merge with the flow of energy and become one with it. By doing this, you will enter a very pleasant state of mind and you could lose track of time, so if time is important, be sure to have a clock or watch you can check periodically. It is also possible to beam to specific areas. Ask to be shown a specific area that is in need of Reiki and slowly scan the client with your hand by moving your hand up and down imagining that your awareness is extended. Allow your intuition and inner awareness to be guided and choose one area. Draw a power symbol over the area and direct the energy to this one spot. To finish, draw a power symbol intending that this seals and completes the treatment. Beaming can be a short treatment in itself, or it can be added to the end of a regular treatment to complete and seal the aura.

Beaming can also be done by counsellors, hypnotherapists, psychologists, and social workers when working with other modalities. This tends to greatly enhance any modality being used. For instance, a hypnotherapist can beam Reiki to the client while the client is in hypnosis. The hypnotherapist simply draws out the distant symbol, then rests the hands in a comfortable position, intending that Reiki flow to the client while they are continuing with the hypnotic session. The same technique can be used by psychologists or other counsellors while talking to the client. It is wise to let the client know at the beginning of the session that you are able to do this and that you will be sending Reiki to them during the session. Those who have used this technique report that it greatly improves the results received by the client. In the case where guided imagery is used, sometimes the client reports experiences where the energy enters their inner experience as a protecting or healing force.

Reiki Mediation. While it is true that Reiki self-treatment is a form of meditation, it is possible to combine doing Reiki on oneself with doing another form of meditation in a very powerful way. This meditation is taught in the ART class. It combines many of the values of other kinds of meditation along with the healing power of Reiki. This meditation is a yantra meditation and is like mantra meditation except that instead of creating a sound or mantra in the mind, we are going to be steadily holding an image in the mind. This meditation can bring physical relaxation, mental clarity including improved ability to visualize and enhanced healing skills. Many have reported improved clairvoyance and the expansion of consciousness. It can also be used to solve problems and achieve goals and has the amazing tendency to surround all the areas of concern in your life with a soft white Reiki mist!

The technique involves steadily holding each of the Reiki symbols in the mind so that the only awareness one has is of the image of the symbol. Start with the power symbols and hold it in the mind for five minutes or longer, then go on to the emotional/mental symbol, the distant symbol and the master symbol. If thoughts arise, gently brush them aside and bring your attention back to the image of the symbol. After doing this, you can then steadily hold an image of a goal you would like to achieve and see it surrounded by the Reiki symbols. Then believe that you have achieved it as you send it up into a field of light overhead. When doing this always state that if this be possible within divine love and wisdom then let it be so. This last affirmation is necessary so that only those things that are in your highest interest will be created.

A more advanced meditation can be done by doing Reiki on yourself as you steadily hold an image of the power symbol on each of the chakra points. Start at the navel and go down to the root chakra and then up to the back to the crown and then down to the navel. Hold the power symbol at each chakra point for 2-3 minutes. After doing this with each chakra, see a beautiful ball of light with the power symbol in it moving down the front through each chakra then up the spine to the top of the head and then down the front - around and around and around. This meditation will harmonize your entire system and transmute all negative energy into positive. It is a great meditation to do whenever you feel out of balance or feel that you may have taken on someone else's negative energy. Both of these meditations are on tape #CT-106, "Bringing in the Light and Creating Balance and Harmony". This tape explains the process and guides you through it. The value of these meditations comes with continual use. Daily practice will develop a strong mind and fill you with peace.

As we move toward the millennium, we are becoming aware of the tremendously positive effect the healing we are doing on ourselves and others is having. We are getting to the point where our individual intentions to heal are merging together to form one planetary purpose. This great purpose is being guided by our own higher selves and is quickened by spiritual beings who send their healing light to us. We are transforming before our very eyes and joining as one. As we do this, there will continue to be more and more wonderful healing techniques and energies shown to us. As we are inspired to use them, we will be more deeply blessed. Let us give thanks for all the love and wonder that is here now for us to enjoy.

THE MOST POWERFUL HAND POSITION

The most powerful hand position is in the form of a T.

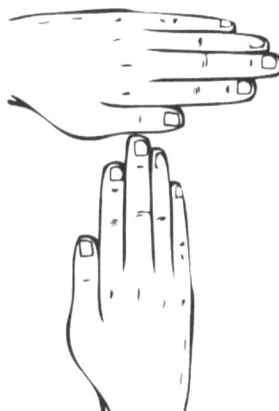

Although this applies for any part of the body, there are two particularly vulnerable spots:
- the head,
- and the soles of the feet.

When holding the head, with one hand holding the Primary Visual Area,
(the occipital bone protuberance, the "bump" at the base of the skull)
and the other hand over the fontanelle (the baby soft spot on top of the head),
everything you think goes straight to the subconscious.

In other words, anything you have on your mind at that time becomes a suggestion to your client. Therefore, it is important to be very clear of your intentions as you are holding this position. A "prayer", asking the Reiki to flow for your client's highest good is most appropriate. The same goes when holding the foot, one hand on the sole of the foot, (your hand chakra covering the foot chakra), the other hand holding the top of the foot being perpendicular to the hand holding the sole of the foot.

I learned this hand position from Donalda Louks when initiated as Tibetan Reiki Master/Teacher in Toronto in early 1996.

The "Psyche" Position - to access Maximum Reiki
by Ellen Louise Kahne

(Source: Reiki News, Winter 1996)

"Psyche" position for treating others

Since Dr. Hayashi developed the Reiki hand positions, variations have arisen through the teaching traditions of different Reiki Masters and their students. A master with whom I studied, Josephine Miranda, taught a unique hand position for Reiki Level II called the "psyche" position. This has proven to be a very valuable tool for all Reiki healers who are familiar with this position.

In treatment, one can use the "psyche" position immediately after the #3 position (hands cradling the back of the head) in the Center's Reiki I & II manual, Reiki: The Healing Touch. The dominant (signing) hand slides out from under the head and is held poised above the crown chakra and the third eye, while the non-dominant hand supports the client's neck and the back of the head. From this position behind the client's head and shoulders, the Reiki practitioner proceeds to sign the mental-emotional symbol, followed by the power symbol over the client's head bringing the signing hand immediately down onto the head, so that the palm of the signing hand covers the crown chakra and the (closed) fingers of that hand extend vertically over the forehead to cover the third eye chakra.

For self-treatment, the non-dominant hand supports the base of the back of the head and the neck, while the dominant (signing) hand is used to sign the mental/emotional symbol and the power symbol over the crown and third eye chakras. Then, the signing hand is placed so that the palm covers the third eye and the (closed) fingers extend vertically across the forehead to cover the crown chakra.

Please note that a practitioner using the "psyche" position should be physically secure and stable, because the quantities of energy accessed through this position can be of such great strength and intensity that one needs to be balanced and steady.

The "psyche" position can be used, and taught as the first position to recall in the case of trauma or life-threatening emergencies. Intuitive abilities notwithstanding, experienced Reiki practitioners and masters who have used this position have found that a person is often able to draw in more Reiki energy immediately through this position than any other hand position, unless one is receiving an attunement. For example, I utilized the "psyche" position to help a neighbor who was having a grand mal epileptic seizure. I witnessed the immediate cessation of the seizure and tremors (the person experienced continuous tremors from parkinsonism), and a subsequent peaceful, Reiki-induced, forty-five minute sleep while awaiting the Emergency Medical Service. A Reiki master whom I know used this position extensively as she stated "more often than my EMS training but in conjunction with it" during her many years of service with a local volunteer ambulance corps.

The "psyche" position can and has been used to access creative abilities and/or information from the deepest recesses of a person's sacred space. I have successfully used this position for clarity and to penetrate writer's and other blocks in myself and others. While in the "psyche" position, a practitioner may receive clarity of insight about oneself, the client or about the Universe. Therefore, the practitioner must be particularly careful to honor the privacy of the Reiki client and to use sensitivity and wisdom in deciding whether to reveal subconscious information, even to the client.

"Psyche" position for self-treatment

Traditionally, the "psyche" position is used in silence. For best results, be open to the "message" which comes through for yourself or your client. For example, you may say (silently) "God embraces you with healing and love" or "You may use this energy to regain control of your vital functions" (in the case of a life-threatening emergency, for example). If you are clairvoyant, a message may be channelled through you when you are in this position, so be open to a positive affirmation or visualization.

When working on mentally or emotionally disabled clients, this position may give the person a few moments of needed serenity and balance, as you visualize a blank screen or the word "Peace". Please note, if your mind begins to wander from your client, your hand slides off the position, or feels like it has been brushed off the client, it is time to continue the treatment in another position. The "psyche" position is an excellent tool to help people conquer addictive behaviors, if this is the desire of the client. The practitioner may be guided to say, silently, "You can use this energy to strengthen your resolve."

The "psyche" position can be used by itself or included with all of the other hand positions and techniques, as part of a complete distance healing treatment. Also, it may be used with the Master symbol, the distance symbol, and/or any of the Karuna symbols in an integrative or solely Karuna treatment for healing past-life or other issues, as the Reiki master or practitioner is guided.

I have successfully integrated the teaching of the "psyche" position into all of my Reiki Level II classes and my Reiki practice. I have found it to be an invaluable tool gained from the cross-fertilization of the very best of our Reiki traditions and our collective wisdom.

Ellen Louise Kahne is a Center Certified Reiki Master Teacher, a Karuna Master and a poet writer and Marathon racewalker, living in New York City.

TRADITIONAL JAPANESE REIKI

The Second Degree

Traditional Japanese Reiki **Second Degree workshop**
Teacher's Checklist
Morning

    [ ] Welcome back
    [ ] Feedback on homework
    [ ] Explain routine
    [ ] Explain the meaning and use of symbols
    [ ] **Attunement to Power Symbol**
                    »»> make them ask for a gift
»»> make them practice hand positions on self
[ ] Feedback »»> "write down your experience"
[ ] Teach Power symbol
        [ ] Name and meaning
        [ ] Origin
        [ ] Use
        [ ] Drawing and pronunciation
[ ] **Attunement to Balance and Harmony Symbol**
                      »»> make them ask for a gift
»»> make them practice hand positions on self
[ ] Feedback »»> "write down your experience"
[ ] Teach Balance and Harmony Symbol
        [ ] Name and meaning
        [ ] Origin
        [ ] Use
        [ ] Drawing and pronunciation

Lunch

- [ ] **Attunement to Distant Healing Symbol**
  - »»> make them ask for a gift
- »»> make them practice hand positions on self
- [ ] Feedback »»> "write down your experience"
- [ ] Teach Power symbol
  - [ ] Name and meaning
  - [ ] Origin
  - [ ] Use
- [ ] Drawing and pronunciation
- [ ] Demonstrate Distant Healing
- [ ] Distant Healing in a group
- [ ] Divide the group in two and
  - [ ] Practice Distant Healing to each other taking turns to experience »»> sending
    - »»> receiving
- [ ] Verbal feedback on Distant Healing
- [ ] Verbal feedback on workshop so far
- [ ] Tomorrow's agenda for 3rd Degree Reiki
  - Starting time - Lunch - Estimated finishing time
- [ ] **Distribute certificates**

THE SYMBOLS

What we call symbols are made of a group of pictograms and present a concept, just like a series of letters of our alphabet make up a word, a concept.

What we call symbols represent words and are written communication.

Japanese give a number to each "symbol," a name, and a mantra (an affirmation), to be repeated three times.

The number and a name of the "symbol" establish our intentions.

The symbol, the scribble, engage our five senses to clarify our intent.

The mantra is an affirmation to clarify our intent at a deeper level. In Japan, the sound as the affirmation is repeated intensifies the intent.
The mantra, the affirmation is always repeated three times or in multiples of three.

We are usually explained that the symbols should be kept secret. In Japan secret means you do not know until you are properly attuned to it. Just like never having baked a cake, it is a secret to you until you are properly instructed, shown how to do it, and then mastered.

THE USE OF THE SYMBOLS

1. Center yourself.
2. Draw the symbol in the air in front of you.
3. Pick it up and pull it over your head as if you wanted to wear it.

At the beginning of a Reiki session, when working with a client or a friend:
    a) Draw the Power Symbol in front of you, pick it up and pull it over yourself
    b) Draw the appropriate symbol in the air in front of you, pick it up and pull over your client / friend.

Note: If client can see what you are doing, mentally draw the symbol and mentally pull the symbol over yourself then mentally draw the symbol and mentally pull the symbol over the client as you gently have your hands on your client / friend.

4. Repeat the mantra three times silently.

#1 Symbol   POWER

Mantra:	CHOKU REI (repeat 3 times or in multiples of 3)
Meaning:	I command the Rei (I command my universe).
	Likely of pre-Tibetan origin, from the country of Bon.

#2 Symbol   HARMONY

Mantra: SEI HEKI (repeat 3 times or in multiples of 3)
Meaning: Balance and Harmony
    Likely Sanskritic, one of the Indic languages developed directly from Sanskrit or the older Vedic. (Vedic: of or related to Vedas, the language with the Veda or Hindu history is written between 1500 B.C. and 500 B.C..)
    Used for emotional and mental harmony.

#3 Symbol   DISTANCE

Mantra: HON SHA ZE SHO NEN (repeat 3 times or in multiples of 3)
Meaning: My spirit sees your spirit. I see you. I acknowledge your presence.
    This is Kanji. Only drawn to bring forth a person living, or deceased, such as for distance healing or to bring a situation past or future, into the present.
    Connects the higher self to events in the past or into the future.
    To prepare a future event or clear the past.

    Always put these symbols over you to empower yourself in any situation, at the beginning of the day, or at the beginning of a session.

DISTANT HEALING

The use of your upper legs.

The use of a Teddy Bear.

The use of a wig stand, etc.

#1 Symbol – POWER

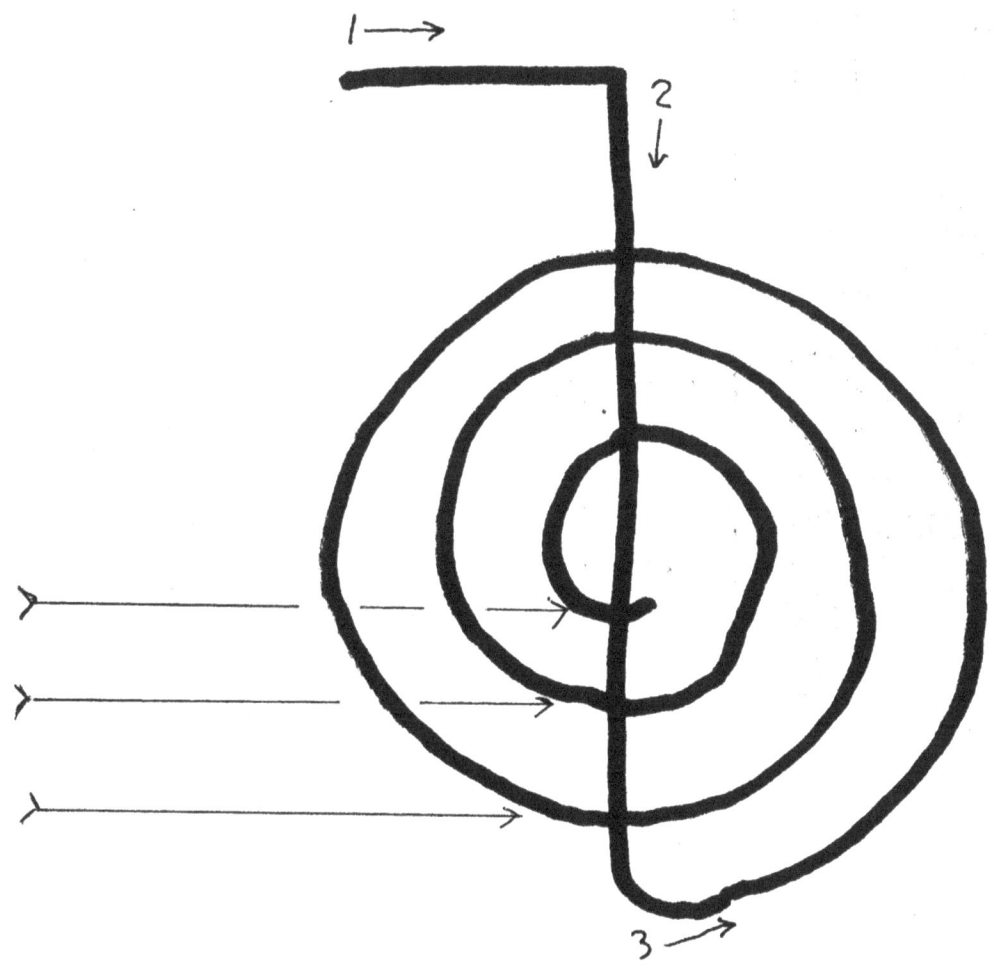

Choku Rei

FIRST – SECOND DEGREE ATTUNEMENT
CHOKU REI

Perform procedure

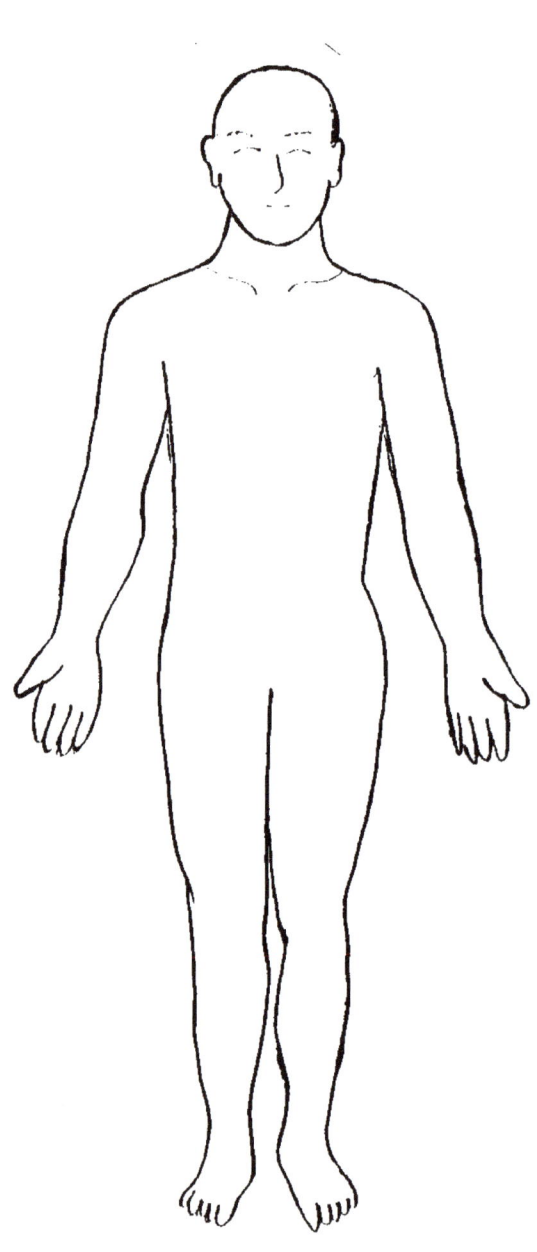

FIRST – SECOND DEGREE ATTUNEMENT CHOKU REI

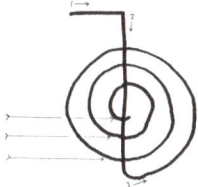

Perform procedure

FIRST – SECOND DEGREE ATTUNEMENT
CHOKU REI

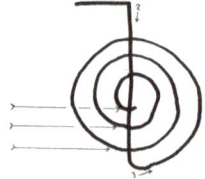

1- Review hand position on self and suggest the students to Reiki themselves after the attunement,

When having left the room, waiting for all the other students to be attuned, the student may Reiki themselves or someone else sitting in the room.

2- Demonstrate on yourself the hand positions during the attunement, and request they put their hands in the prayer position when they feel the Reiki Master/Teacher's hand touching the top of their head.

3- *This is what* *I learned from my first Reiki Master/Teacher:*
Suggest students to ask the Universe a gift, and signal to let you know they decided what gift they are asking for. Once every student got "it", request they now close their eyes and keep their eyes closed until you ask them to open them.

4- Standing behind the student and draw the Master Symbol in the air and move it over your own body.

5- Draw the CHOKU REI in the air repeating the mantra three times and then move it over your client's body.

  - BOW, as to say hello.

  - Clear the student's energy field by making three descending sweeps of the hand from above the student's head to the ground.

  - Place on hand on (or just above) the student's crown chakra and your other hand just above your first hand. **Perform procedure.**

  - Place your hands on the student's shoulders and **perform procedure.**

- Move to the left side of the student and place your left hand on the student's forehead and your right hand on t6he student's occiput and **perform procedure.**

- Sit/kneel/stand in front of the student and place your hands on the student's ankles, just below the ankle bone, and **perform procedure.**

- Sit/kneel/stand in front of the student and place your hands over the student's hands held in prayer and **perform procedure**.

- Sit/kneel/stand in front of the student and open/separate the student's hands.

FIRST – SECOND DEGREE ATTUNEMENT
CHOKU REI

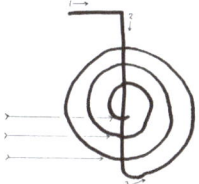

- Place one hand slightly below the student's right hand and with your other hand write the CHOKU REI over the palm of their hand three times repeating the mantra as you put your other hand over the palm of their hand "sandwiching" the palm, and **perform procedure**.

- Place one hand slightly below the student's left hand and with your other hand write the CHOKU REI over the palm of their hand three times repeating the mantra as you put your other hand over the palm of their hand "sandwiching" the palm, and **perform procedure**.

- Stand in front of the student and place the student's hands back into the prayers position and blow gently and continuously along the space between the hands, going from the thumb side palm to the little finger side palm <u>with the intention of sealing the initiation into the palm of the hands.</u> Rotate the student's hands while doing so.

- Still holding the student's hands, give a short, sharp blast of breath to the student's crown chakra, heart chakra and the dantien chakra (just below the navel).

- *This is my idea*: Still holding the student's hands, I silently wish them "to heal, clear, resolve and dissolve, whatever has to be healed, cleared resolved and dissolved".

- Go behind the student **and draw the CHOKU REI** in the air repeating the mantra three times and then move it over your client's body.

- Make a single upward sweep of the hand, from the floor to above the student's head, (as to close the door).

- Bow, as to say 'goodbye'.

- Take the student's right hand and place it on the student's left shoulder.

- Take the student's leftt hand and place it on the student's right shoulder.

- Place your hands on the student's shoulders and give them a gentle tug.

6 - When the initiations are completed, ask the student(s) to open their eyes stay silent and in the privacy of their own self write down their experience.

#2 Symbol – HARMONY

Sei Heki

Variations		
Kiliku As found in Mikkyo Temples	Indic	Japanese

SECOND – SECOND DEGREE ATTUNEMENT
SEI HEKI

Perform procedure

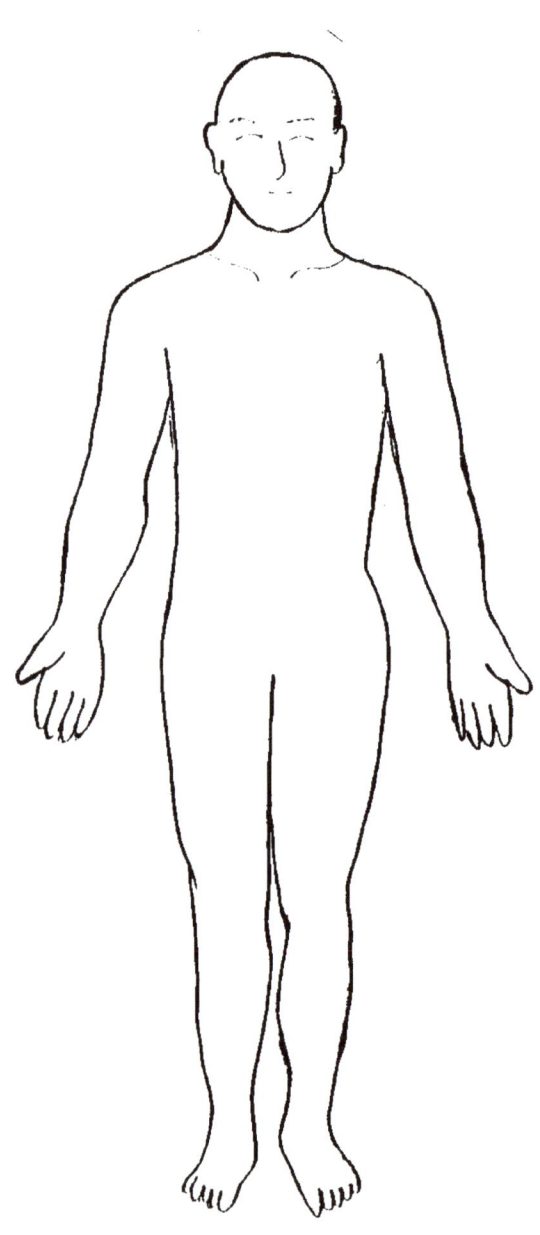

SECOND – SECOND DEGREE ATTUNEMENT
SEI HEKI

Perform procedure

SECOND – SECOND DEGREE ATTUNEMENT
SEI HEKI

1- Review hand position on self and suggest the students to Reiki themselves after the attunement,

When having left the room, waiting for all the other students to be attuned, the student may Reiki themselves or someone else sitting in the room.

2- Demonstrate on yourself the hand positions during the attunement, and request they put their hands in the prayer position when they feel the Reiki Master/Teacher's hand touching the top of their head.

3- *This is what* *I learned from my first Reiki Master/Teacher:*
Suggest students to ask the Universe a gift, and signal to let you know they decided what gift they are asking for. Once every student got "it", request they now close their eyes and keep their eyes closed until you ask them to open them.

4- Standing behind the student and draw the Master Symbol in the air and move it over your own body.

5- Draw the SEI HEKI in the air repeating the mantra three times and then move it over your client's body.

- BOW, as to say hello.

- Clear the student's energy field by making three descending sweeps of the hand from above the student's head to the ground.

- Place on hand on (or just above) the student's crown chakra and your other hand just above your first hand. **Perform procedure.**

- Place your hands on the student's shoulders and **perform procedure.**

- Move to the left side of the student and place your left hand on the student's forehead and your right hand on t6he student's occiput and **perform procedure.**

- Sit/kneel/stand in front of the student and place your hands on the student's ankles, just below the ankle bone, and **perform procedure.**

- Sit/kneel/stand in front of the student and place your hands over the student's hands held in prayer and **perform procedure**.

- Sit/kneel/stand in front of the student and open/separate the student's hands.

SECOND – SECOND DEGREE ATTUNEMENT
SEI HEKI

- Place one hand slightly below the student's right hand and with your other hand write the **SEI HEKI** over the palm of their hand three times repeating the mantra as you put your other hand over the palm of their hand "sandwiching" the palm, and **perform procedure**.

- Place one hand slightly below the student's left hand and with your other hand write the **SEI HEKI** over the palm of their hand three times repeating the mantra as you put your other hand over the palm of their hand "sandwiching" the palm, and **perform procedure**.

- Stand in front of the student and place the student's hands back into the prayers position and blow gently and continuously along the space between the hands, going from the thumb side palm to the little finger side palm **with the intention of sealing the initiation into the palm of the hands.** Rotate the student's hands while doing so.

- Still holding the student's hands, give a short, sharp blast of breath to the student's crown chakra, heart chakra and the dantien chakra (just below the navel).

- *This is my idea*: Still holding the student's hands, I silently wish them "to heal, clear, resolve and dissolve, whatever has to be healed, cleared resolved and dissolved".

- Go behind the student **and draw the SEI HEKI** in the air repeating the mantra three times and then move it over your client's body.

- Make a single upward sweep of the hand, from the floor to above the student's head, (as to close the door).

- Bow, as to say 'goodbye'.

- Take the student's right hand and place it on the student's left shoulder.

- Take the student's left hand and place it on the student's right shoulder.

- Place your hands on the student's shoulders and give them a gentle tug.

6 - When the initiations are completed, ask the student(s) to open their eyes stay silent and in the privacy of their own self write down their experience.

#3 Symbol – DISTANCE

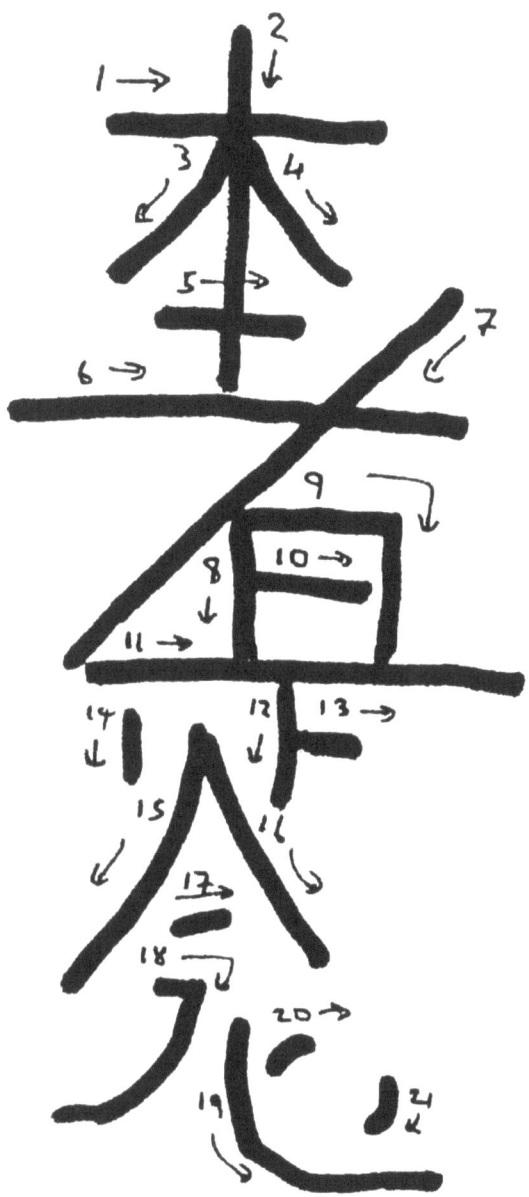

Hon Sha Ze Sho Nen

#3 Symbol – DISTANCE

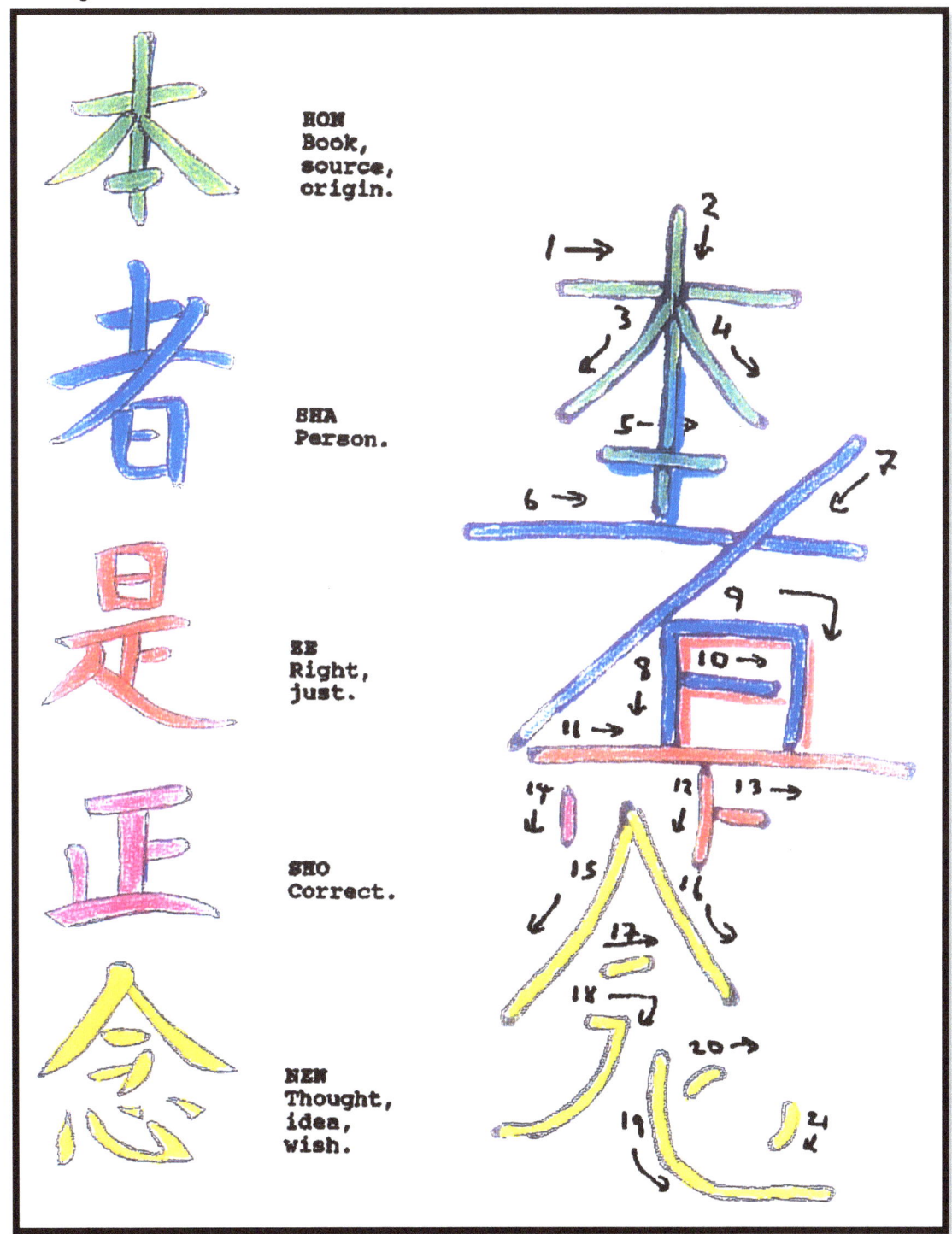

Hon Sha Ze Sho Nen

(Image: Scan of a hand coloured page from Anny's personal Reiki book)

THIRD – SECOND DEGREE ATTUNEMENT
HON SHA ZE SHO NEN

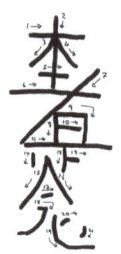

Perform procedure

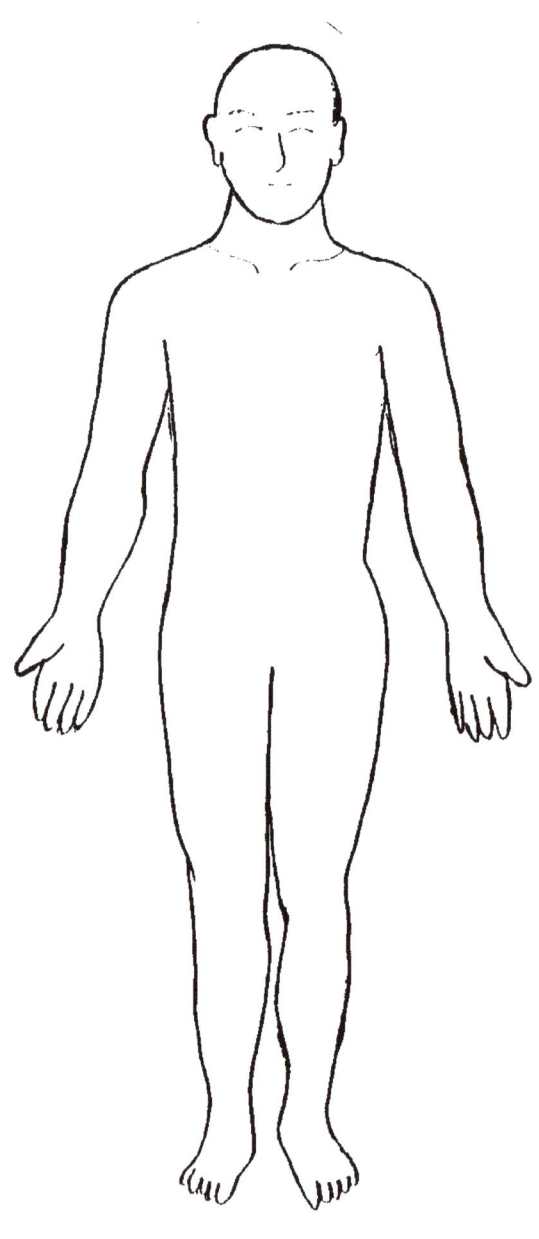

THIRD – SECOND DEGREE ATTUNEMENT
HON SHA ZE SHO NEN

Perform procedure

THIRD – SECOND DEGREE ATTUNEMENT
HON SHA ZE SHO NEN

1- Review hand position on self and suggest the students to Reiki themselves after the attunement,

When having left the room, waiting for all the other students to be attuned, the student may Reiki themselves or someone else sitting in the room.

2- Demonstrate on yourself the hand positions during the attunement, and request they put their hands in the prayer position when they feel the Reiki Master/Teacher's hand touching the top of their head.

3- *This is what* I learned from my first Reiki Master/Teacher:
Suggest students to ask the Universe a gift, and signal to let you know they decided what gift they are asking for. Once every student got "it", request they now close their eyes and keep their eyes closed until you ask them to open them.

4- Standing behind the student and draw the Master Symbol in the air and move it over your own body.

5- Draw the HON SHA ZE SHO NEN in the air repeating the mantra three times and then move it over your client's body.

  - BOW, as to say hello.

  - Clear the student's energy field by making three descending sweeps of the hand from above the student's head to the ground.

  - Place on hand on (or just above) the student's crown chakra and your other hand just above your first hand. **Perform procedure.**

  - Place your hands on the student's shoulders and **perform procedure.**

- Move to the left side of the student and place your left hand on the student's forehead and your right hand on t6he student's occiput and **perform procedure.**

- Sit/kneel/stand in front of the student and place your hands on the student's ankles, just below the ankle bone, and **perform procedure.**

- Sit/kneel/stand in front of the student and place your hands over the student's hands held in prayer and **perform procedure**.

- Sit/kneel/stand in front of the student and open/separate the student's hands.

THIRD – SECOND DEGREE ATTUNEMENT
HON SHA ZE SHO NEN

- Place one hand slightly below the student's right hand and with your other hand write the **HON SHA ZE SHO NEN** over the palm of their hand three times repeating the mantra as you put your other hand over the palm of their hand "sandwiching" the palm, and **perform procedure**.

- Place one hand slightly below the student's left hand and with your other hand write the **HON SHA ZE SHO NEN** over the palm of their hand three times repeating the mantra as you put your other hand over the palm of their hand "sandwiching" the palm, and **perform procedure**.

- Stand in front of the student and place the student's hands back into the prayers position and blow gently and continuously along the space between the hands, going from the thumb side palm to the little finger side palm **with the intention of sealing the initiation into the palm of the hands.** Rotate the student's hands while doing so.

- Still holding the student's hands, give a short, sharp blast of breath to the student's crown chakra, heart chakra and the dantien chakra (just below the navel).

- *This is my idea*: Still holding the student's hands, I silently wish them "to heal, clear, resolve and dissolve, whatever has to be healed, cleared resolved and dissolved".

- Go behind the student **and draw the HON SHA ZE SHO NEN** in the air repeating the mantra three times and then move it over your client's body.

- Make a single upward sweep of the hand, from the floor to above the student's head, (as to close the door).

- Bow, as to say 'goodbye'.

- Take the student's right hand and place it on the student's left shoulder.

- Take the student's left hand and place it on the student's right shoulder.

- Place your hands on the student's shoulders and give them a gentle tug.

6 - When the initiations are completed, ask the student(s) to open their eyes stay silent and in the privacy of their own self write down their experience.

TRADITIONAL JAPANESE REIKI

The Third Degree

Traditional Japanese Reiki **Third Degree Workshop** Teacher's Checklist

Morning

[ ] Welcome back
[ ] Explain routine - Same attunement 3 times
[ ] **First attunement to Master Symbol**

Remember to *pass on the joy of it all*

»»> make them ask for a gift
»»> make them practice hand positions on self
[ ] Feedback »»> "write down your experience"
[ ] Teach Master symbol
[ ] Name and meaning
[ ] Origin
[ ] Use
[ ] Drawing and pronunciation
[ ] **Second attunement to Master Symbol**
»»> make them ask for a gift
»»> make them practice hand positions on self
[ ] Feedback »»> "write down your experience"
[ ] Meditation on the Symbols

Lunch

[ ] Demonstration Chakra balancing
[ ] Practice Chakra balancing
[ ] Practice of all the symbols
[ ] Discussion - any aspect of Reiki learned so far

[ ] **Third attunement to Master Symbol**
  »»> make them ask for a gift
  »»> make them practice hand positions on self
[ ] Verbal feedback on their experience
[ ] Presentation of the symbols to the group
[ ] Verbal feedback on workshop
[ ] **Distribute certificates**

This book was originally Cerlox bonded, allowing me to add the Third-Degree Reiki information only when the student was taking the third degree as part of the Reiki course.

After serious soul searching – it is with peace of mind that I decided to add the Third Degree information for all to see – including the "Master Symbol" in this book.

The reason?

As explained in my book Volume II:
Reiki Ryoho Hikkei
(The Most Important Methods for Reiki)
I was introduced to a Japanese Scholar who enlightened me about the Japanese culture.

When visiting her, I had with me two books about Reiki I had ordered from Japan that included a thick binder with photocopies which advertised the Reiki courses.

The Scholar was translating what she was reading at an amazing speed, starting from what we consider the back page of the book up and down and from right to left, holding a pointer.

When she started to translate the advertisement, I realised the number of initiations per each "symbol" were also given. I had also noticed that the advertising contained the pictures of the complete rituals when doing initiations.

Before learning the way that Reiki was being taught in Japan, I had learned that the "symbols" were secret (and should be kept that way).

The nine Reiki courses I reviewed by teachers of the Reiki Alliance (and one from my first Reiki course given by an Independent Reiki Master Teacher), all explained the symbols were secret and only memorised – so no one could see them.

Anything written had to be erased or burned.

The Scholar explained to me that in Japan, a secret means something you do not know. For example: If you to not know Kanji, Kanji is a secret to you. Never boiled potatoes. Then, boiling potatoes is a secret to you.

Therefore, no matter how much you read or see about the affirmations commonly know as symbols, or even the initiation rituals, it stays a mystery to you. This is because unless you are properly trained, you have absolutely no idea of the work involved during all the rituals. This includes reciting the mantras, the affirmations, and giving Reiki sessions.

With Love and Light,

Anny Slegten

#4 Symbol – MASTER

Mantra: DAI KO MYO (repeat 3 times or in multiples of 3)
Meaning: Great Strength of the Universe, Shine Upon Me.
Kanji.

    Used only and always to empower yourself.
    Once you have received this symbol, this is the only one you will use for yourself.

1. Center yourself.

2. Draw the Master symbol big, in front of you.

    One second for each stroke.

    Watch your intent: it is to empower yourself.

3. Pick it up and "put it on".

大光明	大光明
Traditional Brush Painted.	*Modern Computer Typeface*

#4 Symbol – MASTER

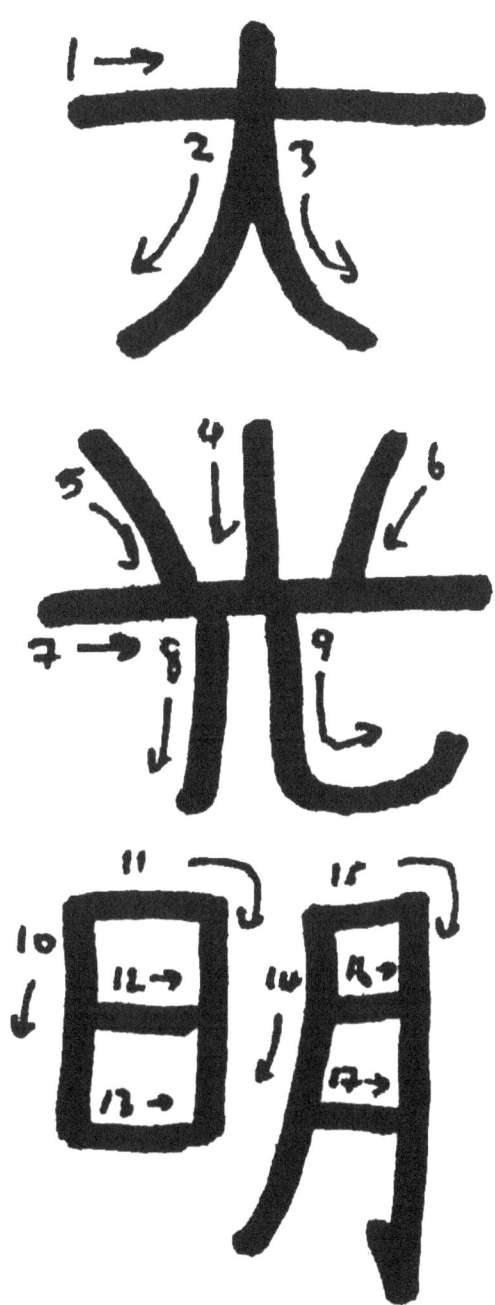

Dai Kō Myo

THIRD DEGREE ATTUNEMENT
DAI KO MIO

Perform procedure

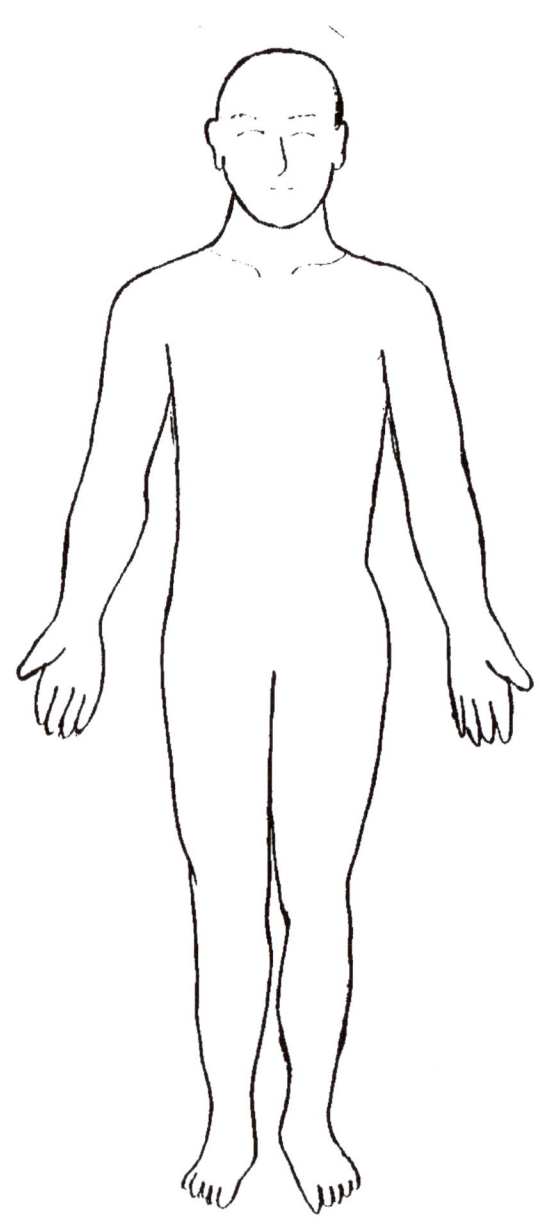

THIRD DEGREE ATTUNEMENT
DAI KO MIO

Perform procedure

THIRD DEGREE ATTUNEMENT
DAI KO MIO

1- Explain to student the initiation is almost the same as before, and suggest to Reiki themselves after the attunement, or Reiki someone else sitting in a chair/laying on table.

2- Remind student to hold their hands in the prayer position and keep their eyes closed until you signal or ask them to open their eyes.

3- *Reiki Master Trish Dennison's way: suggest student* to *ask the Universe for* a *gift*.

4- Stand behind the student and draw the MASTER SYMBOL in the air repeating the mantra three times, and move it over your own body.

- Draw the DAI KO MYO in the air over the student's head, repeating the mantra three times, and move it over the student's head and back.

- Clear the student's energy by making three descending sweeps of the hands from above the student's head to the ground.

- Place one hand on (or just above) the student's crown chakra and your other hand just above your first hands. Perform procedure *.

- Place your hands on the student's shoulders and perform procedure *.

- Move to the left side of the student and place your left hand on the student's forehead and your right hand on the student's occiput and perform procedure *.

- Sit/kneel in front of the student and place your hands on the student's ankles, just below the ankle bone, and perform procedure*.

- Sit/kneel/stand in front of the student and place your hands over the student's hands held in prayer and perform procedure *.

- Stand in front of the student and open/separate the student's hands.

- Place one hand slightly below the student's right hand and with your other hand draw the DAI KO MYO over the palm of their hand three times, repeating the mantra as you do so, and then perform procedure*

THIRD DEGREE ATTUNEMENT
DAI KO MIO

- Move your hand slightly below the student's left hand and with your other hand draw the DAI KO MYO over the palm of their hand three times, repeating
the mantra as you do so, and then perform procedure*

- Stand in front of student and place the student's hands back into the prayer position and blow gently and continuously along the space between the hands going from the thumb side palm to little finger side palm <u>with the intention of sealing the DAI KO MYO into the student's palm of their hands</u>. Rotate the student's hands while doing so.

- Still holding the student's hands, give a short, sharp blast of breath to the student's crown chakra, heart chakra and dantien chakra (just below the navel).

- *This is my idea: Still holding the student's hands, I then silently wish something specially for them.*

- Go behind the student and draw the DAI KO MYO in the air over the student's head, repeating the mantra three times, and move it over the student's head and back.

- Make a single upward sweep from the floor to above the student's head.

Bow.

- Take the student's right hand and place it on, the student's left shoulder.

- Take the student's left hand and place it on the student's right shoulder.

- Place your hands on the student's shoulders and give them a gentle tug.

5- When the initiation is completed, ask the student(s) to open their eyes.

I then ask the student(s) to write down their experience.

The Reiki Master Symbol

One of the Japanese Alphabets is called Kanji. The word Kanji means "Chinese characters" and as this suggests, China is where Japanese Kanji originated.

Each character can have several meanings depending on the context. The Kanji on this page come from "Essential Kanji" by P.G. O'Neill, courtesy William Rand.

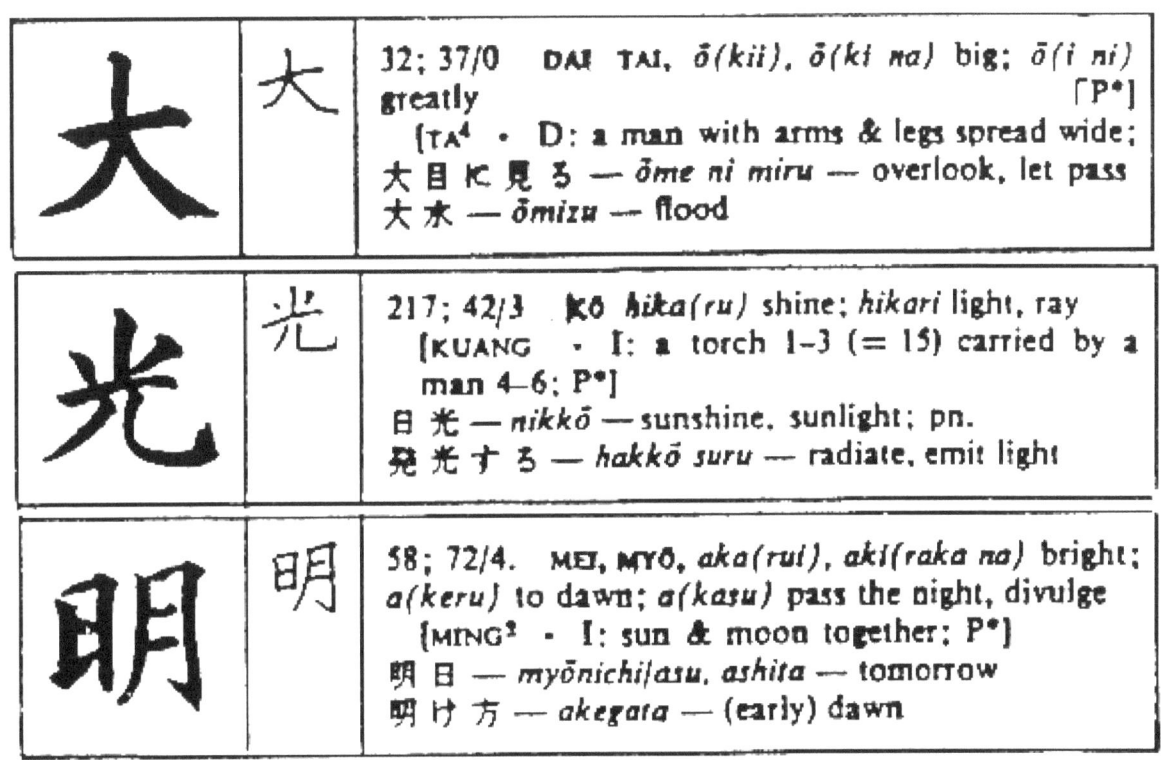

Reiki News

Published by the Center for Reiki Training - Southfield, Michigan, U.S.A.

Advanced Reiki Techniques - Part II
by William Lee Rand

The mass awakening toward higher consciousness and personal growth which started in the 60's has continually gained momentum. As each of us continues to work on personal healing, not only do we contribute to our own well-being, but the influence we have on those around us, helps them to grow as well. This synergistic effect allows the pace of our improvement to quicken even more. As healers work on each other and share their skills, a higher level of possibility for all of us is created. It must be remembered that the universe is a limitless reservoir of possibilities. To improve your healing skills, an open mind and a willingness to try new techniques is necessary. This article describes methods for intensifying and extending your Reiki healing energies. These techniques are taught in the Advanced Reiki Training class.

Crystals and Continuous Healing

One thing necessary for Reiki to work is your intention. You must intend for Reiki to flow in order to start it flowing. This can be a conscious or an unconscious intention and is often accompanied by placing your hands on someone. Quartz crystal has the unique property of being able to absorb and hold thoughts and intentions. Because of this, it is possible to place your intention as well as your ability to transmit Reiki into a crystal so that the crystal will continue to send Reiki while you are doing other things. This is valuable if you have someone you are working on who is really in need.

Each crystal has its own vibration and there will be some crystals that are available to you that are better suited for use in sending distant Reiki than others. So the first step is to choose a crystal that is appropriate to use with Reiki. This can be done using your intuition or through the use of a pendulum or with muscle testing or some other method of accessing your inner knowing. After you have chosen a crystal, or in some cases after the crystal has chosen you, it is often necessary to clean the crystal of any inappropriate energy it may have. You can check if this is needed with your pendulum or using any of the methods mentioned above. If it is indicated that the crystal needs cleansing, then simply place it in a bowl of rock or sea salt making sure it is covered with salt. Then do Reiki over the bowl of salt asking that the crystal be cleansed and blessed for your intended use with distant Reiki. Then leave it for 24 hours. All vibrations will be removed and you will then have a completely neutral crystal. There are many other ways to clean a crystal such as placing it under running water, placing it in the ground outside so the sun and moon will shine on it, placing it in salt water, smudging it, or doing Reiki on it with the intention of cleansing it. Use the method that feels right for you and the crystal.

After it is cleansed, it will be necessary to charge it with Reiki. Simply hold it between your hands and draw the distant symbols over it and do Reiki on it intending that the crystal will be charged with your ability to send distant Reiki. You can also visualize any other Reiki symbols you have use of entering the crystal. Steadily hold the image of each symbol in the crystal. Include a prayer asking that the original Reiki master bless your crystal and your intention to help and to heal others through its use.

After this initial process of cleansing and blessing, your crystal will be ready for use. There are several methods you can use to send distant Reiki continuously through your crystal, but they are all very similar. Simply take a picture of the person or if you don't have a picture, you can write the person's name on a piece of paper. Then place the paper in your hand and place the crystal over it. Draw the distant symbol over the crystal and picture or name and say the name of the distant symbols three times intending that a Reiki connection be established. You can also add any other Reiki symbols you feel appropriate at this time. Then place both hands over the crystal and picture or name and begin doing Reiki intending that it be sent to the person. While you are doing Reiki, intend that the crystal will absorb your ability to send distant Reiki and that it will send it continuously. After sending Reiki in this way for 10 to 20 minutes or so (it could be longer if you have the time), set the picture or name down and place the crystal on top. Then draw out the distant Reiki symbol again over the crystal and picture or name and then draw out the power symbol. As you do this, intend that Reiki will continuously flow to the person for as long as it is needed or is valuable. If you have done this with a loving purpose, Reiki will continue to flow to the person for many hours or even days if it is needed. It can also be helpful to reaffirm your intention each day by following the above steps again. This process can also be used with a situation or with goals. Just write out a description of the situation or goal on a piece of paper and follow the same steps. The blessings that will come to those you send distant Reiki to by using this process will be truly wonderful. Also, any goals or situations you send to will also be blessed with love, new guidance and accomplishment.

The Reiki Grid

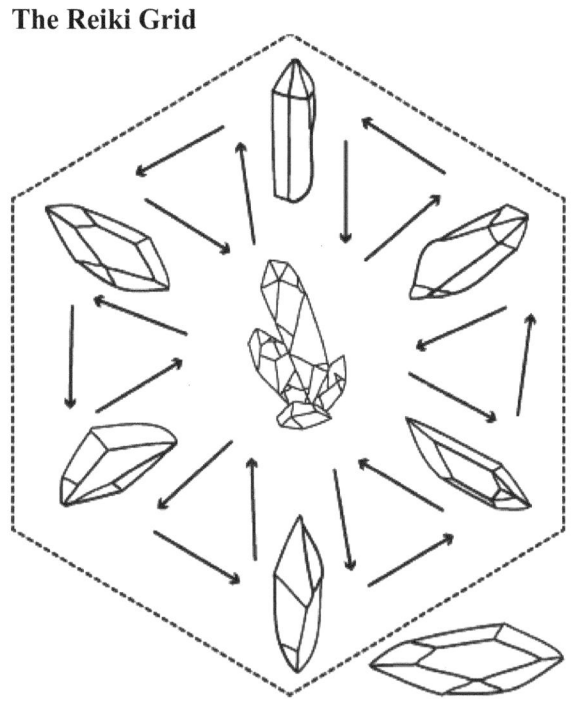

It is possible to create a grid or pattern using eight crystals and charge them with Reiki energy so they will continuously send Reiki to yourself or anyone whose picture or name you place in the grid. This advanced technique is more effective than the use of a single crystal and can be used to send Reiki to many people and situations at the same time.

The beginning steps are similar to those necessary for using a single crystal. First, choose your eight crystals asking for guidance in finding those that would work best in your Reiki grid. You will need six crystals for the outside part of the grid, one for the center and one to use as a master crystal. The center crystal can be a single or a double terminated crystal, a crystal pyramid or a crystal ball or a crystal cluster. The master crystal needs to be a longer crystal like a laser or one with more of a yang or male type energy. It is also possible to use other kinds of crystals besides quartz or other stones. Always check with your pendulum or other method to be sure that any crystals or stones you choose will work and that they are willing to be used in the Reiki grid. Then cleanse them if they need it and charge them in the same manner as above.

Once they are charged, arrange the six outer crystals in a hexagram about eight to twelve or so inches across with the points pointing toward the center. Place the central crystal in the middle with the point going between two of the outer crystals. The master crystal is placed outside the grid, off to the side. (See diagram)

Take a picture of yourself and place it in the middle under the central crystal. On the back of the picture, write out a positive open-ended affirmation such as, "The love and wisdom of God guides and empowers me to fulfill my life purpose" or "I am completely healed by God's love and wisdom now". Or you could also create your own positive affirmation.

It is a good idea to place your grid on a piece of stiff cardboard so that you can move it around if you need to. Also, after you have charged each crystal, it is also helpful to glue each crystal down to the cardboard with a small amount of rubber cement so they will not move around. Keep your grid in a sacred place that is private.

You will need to charge your Reiki grid each day to keep it empowered. To do this, take the master crystal and hold it between your hands. Then draw the distant symbols over it and any other symbols you are guided to use such as the power symbol or the master symbol.

Then do Reiki on the master crystal for 5-10 minutes to charge it with Reiki. As you do this you can also pray to your guides or angels or other spiritual beings to work with you and to charge the master crystal with love and deep healing. Once the master crystal is charged, go over to your Reiki grid and use the master crystal to draw out the distant symbol over the Reiki grid. Also draw out any other symbols you feel guided to use. Then point the master crystal at the central crystal and begin moving it out to one of the outer crystals, then move it over to the crystal next to it, then move it back to the central crystal again, then back out to the same outer crystal, then move over one more crystal and in and out and continue directing the energy of the master crystal in and out and around and around. As you do this, you will be moving in and out, then over one crystal, then in and out, then over one crystal, then in and out, then over, etc. as though you are cutting out pieces of pie. You will be moving around the grid as you do this. You can go either way, clockwise or counter-clockwise depending on how you are guided. Go around at least eight or ten times or more. (See diagram)

As you charge your Reiki grid with your master crystal, say a continuous series of affirmations or prayers such as, "I charge this grid with light, with light, with light, to heal, to heal, to heal. I charge this grid with Reiki, with Reiki, with Reiki, to heal, to heal, to heal." You can also add, "I connect this Reiki grid to my highest spiritual guides to heal, to heal, to heal, I connect this grid to the power of God, to heal, to heal, to heal." Say this over and over also.

Then, once it is charged, anyone whose name or picture you place in the grid, will continuously receive distant Reiki. You can also place your goals or other situations on a piece of paper and they will be blessed with Reiki also.

It will be necessary for you to charge your Reiki grid each day to keep it working. Doing this is like a meditation as each time you charge it, you will feel like you are being charged with energy and becoming more focused as well. Because your picture is in the middle, you will also be receiving a continuous blessing of Reiki all day long.

If you go away and still want to keep your grid charged, take a photograph of your grid. Take the photo with you when you travel along with the master crystal. Then, using the distant symbol, connect with your grid through the picture and charge it using your master crystal. This will keep your grid charged and the picture itself will have an energy around it and be very healing and protective for your to carry with you during your travels.

As we continue to receive additional training and to follow our inner guidance, not just for healing individual issues, but for the healing and guidance of our lives, we become more a part of the great transformation that is taking place on the planet. The upward flow of Reiki is growing continually stronger as more people on the planet are being attuned to this compassionate healing power. Do not hold back, but allow yourself to surrender completely to this upward flow of healing love. Then you will know what it means to truly be alive and to be free.

Summer 1996 Reiki News

Reiki News

Published by the Center for Reiki Training - Southfield, Michigan, U.S.A.

Advanced Reiki Techniques - Part III
Reiki and Psychic Surgery

by William Lee Rand

We all have dormant abilities inside ourselves waiting to be used. The ability to heal ourselves and each other is one of those abilities. It is simply a matter of claiming your power and developing the skill to use it. Psychic surgery is a tool that allows you to take charge of your inner power and use it to heal.

I developed this psychic surgery technique based on training I received from a Kahuna while living in Hawaii. I took a technique I learned from him and after meditating on it and asking for help from my guides, combined it with Reiki energy. This technique is taught in Advanced Reiki Training and is easily learned in class with the help of a Center Certified Reiki Master. By carefully following these instructions, you will be able to do psychic surgery on yourself or your clients with powerful results.

The main reason people are not in optimum health is because they attract or create blocks to the flow of life force energy within themselves. These blocks are usually made of old ideas, beliefs and emotions that are opposed to the persons maximum well-being. They are usually created from misunderstandings about how to get ones needs met in a healthy way. Blocks to life force energy usually take on a particular shape and lodge themselves in or around the organs of the body or in the chakras or auras. These negative energy blocks can cause health problems as well as other difficulties in life. Once they are removed, the life force energy returns to its normal healthy flow and the persons health is restored. Psychic surgery can be used to release these negative energy blocks. This process can assist in the healing of any problem or difficulty including emotional difficulties, relationship problems, addictions, spiritual problems as well as physical health problems. It must be kept in mind that if a person has a physical or psychological problem, it is important for you to advise them to see a licensed health care provider and to let them know that the purpose or your treatment is to work in conjunction with regular medical or psychological care.

Psychic surgery can be done by itself or in conjunction with a regular Reiki session with psychic surgery being done first or even during a regular session. You can also so do this technique on yourself. This type of psychic surgery works with the energy field in and around a person. It does not actually cut open the body or remove physical tissue as is done with psychic surgery in the Philippines.

The first step is to find the location of the block and what it looks like. This is actually easier to do than you might think. Ask the client to close their eyes and to meditate on the issue. It is not necessary for the practitioner to know what the problem is, and this can be helpful as some issues are too sensitive or embarrassing for the person to actually talk about. Once they are focused on the issue, ask them, "if the cause of the problem were in some part of the physical body, where would it be?" If the person feels tension in a part of their body when they think about the problem, than this would be the location to choose. If they have a physical problem, then often but not always, the cause can be at or near the location of the physical symptoms. If they have any trouble at all, just ask them to use their imagination and follow their feelings. There is no wrong answer and simply guessing often works just fine.

After the location has been found, have the client focus on the spot and ask them, "if the cause of this problem had a shape, what shape would it have?" It could have any shape such as a cube, a sphere, a pyramid, a blob, broken pieces of glass, little spots or any other shape. Whatever shape they choose is fine. Then ask them, "if the shape had a color or colors what would they be?" Then ask, "If you could feel its surface, what texture would it have?" It could be smooth, slippery, rough or bumpy or some other texture. Then ask, "how heavy is it, how much does it weigh?" Then ask, "If it could make a sound or say something, what sound would it make or what would it say?"

After they get most or all of these answers, the cause will now have a nonverbal identity that the client will be consciously aware of. This is important because often a person will have only a vague impression of the cause. This process gives the client something to focus on and by having a location, shape, color, texture, weight and sound, for the cause, the person will be more connected to the nonverbal, energetic attributes of the cause and will be able to monitor its condition as you proceed with your healing work.

If a physical organ is affected, the cause will not look like the physical organ, but will be a shape attached to the physical organ or it could be somewhere else in the body. Also, there is sometimes more than one location and if that is the case, it is important to work with the most important location first and then deal with the others after that if they are still present.

To prepare for psychic surgery, first draw the Usui Master and Power symbols on the palms of your hands.
- see drawing #1.
(If you don't have a master symbol, just use the power symbol. You can also add any other symbols you have and are guided to use.) Then draw the power symbol down the front of your body and on each of the seven chakras intending this process to empower and protect you. Then say a prayer calling on the help of your highest Reiki guides, your angels, the ascended masters and any other spiritual beings or guides who you feel will be helpful.

Then extend your Reiki fingers
- see drawing #2
This is done by grabbing hold of your fingers with one hand, imagining they are made of taffy or some other malleable substance and imagine that you are stretching them out about 12" to 18" or so. As you do this, breathe in through pursed lips making an audible sound. Do this several times. Then draw a power symbol on the ends of the extended fingers and tap them to affirm they are extended and have substance. Do this with both hands.

Psychic surgery is done with your full focus and intention. It is much like a martial art and done with your entire being. Using your physical, emotional, mental and spiritual senses. It is done with complete confidence in your ability, knowing that Reiki is all powerful and that you will succeed. Note: that it is your focused intention through which your guides will be able to work, so keep your intention clear and strong. This will be created in part by your posture. So when doing psychic surgery, keep your posture confident, definite, and clear so that there is no question about what you are doing.

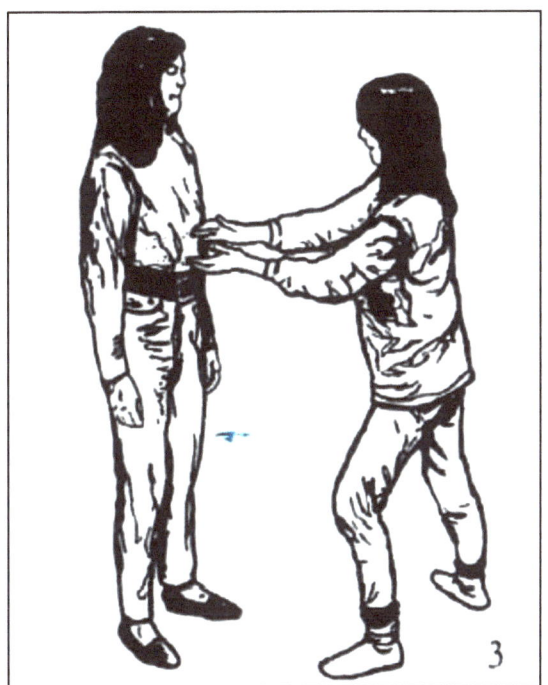

You are now ready to begin. The client can be sitting or standing or laying on a Reiki table. Ask them where the cause is located in the body and what its shape, color, texture, weight, sound etc. is. Ask them to focus on the area and be willing to let go of the shape and be healed. Then draw a power symbol over the area to act as a focal point and to energize the area. Stand next to the person and focus on the area. Then using your hands imagine reaching in with your extended Reiki fingers and imagine pulling out the shape and sending it up to your guides and to the light.

- see drawings 3-5. As you pull the shape out, breathe in through pursed lips making an audible sound. As you send the energy up, breathe out making an audible sound. It is important to imagine that as you pull the shape out, you are breathing into your hands and pulling the negative energy only into the hands. Then breathe out from your hands as you send the negative energy up to your guides and the light. It is not necessary to actually see the shape, when pulling it out (although you may sometimes see it). Simply intend that the process is working and that you are removing the cause of the problem.

Do this process over and over five to ten times or more- reaching in, pulling out the shape, and sending it up to the light. As you do this, you may notice a change in how the energy feels and you may feel guided to expand the area you are pulling from or to work in a somewhat different way. Sometimes you will be guided to pull from the back in addition to pulling from the front.

After doing this a while, stop and ask

the client how they feel and ask them to describe what the shape looks like now. They may say that the shape has completely gone. If so then ask them to look very carefully all around inside to be sure that it is completely gone. If there is still some of the shape left, continue doing psychic surgery, periodically asking what the shape looks like and continuing with this process until it is completely gone.

After the shape is gone, do Reiki on the location to fill it with light and complete the healing - see drawing #6. Then step back, make a karate chop in the air between the two of you to break any psychic cord(s) that may have formed. Also, retract your Reiki fingers by pushing them back into your physical fingers with your hand while making a blowing sound.

Most psychic blocks can be easily removed using this process. However, if after doing several sets of psychic surgery, you find that the shape has not changed or has changed very little or if it seems there is some resistance, then it is likely that the cause of the problem has something to communicate to the client before it will be willing to leave. There may be a lesson the client needs to learn, and it may be necessary for the client to interact consciously with the cause in order for it to heal.

If you feel this is the case, draw mental/emotional symbol over the area and do Reiki there. As you do Reiki, talk directly to the cause and let it know that you respect the information it has to offer and that you are ready to hear what it has to say now. Ask it to tell you what it needs to do in order to heal. Then ask the client to tell you whatever comes into their mind, even if it seems like nonsense. You can also start verbalizing whatever comes into your mind. At first it may not make sense, but ask the client to tell you if anything you say has any meaning or connection to the problem and if it causes any feelings or emotions to come up. Ask them to tell you if they get any meaningful ideas about it too. You could get ideas like: "I need to let go of anger toward my mother." Or, "I feel guilty about the way I treated my younger brother when I was growing up, I need to forgive myself for what I did." Or, "I feel jealous about a friend who is successful and I need to let go of this." You could get ideas like this or something completely different or unique. However, let the client decide what feels right and what makes sense to them concerning what feelings come up and what they need to do to complete the healing.

After you get an idea of what the client needs to do, ask them if they would be willing to do it right now. If they say yes, then continue to do Reiki on the area. I ask them to take some time to focus on the area and the issue and to process letting go of the anger, or forgiving themselves, or releasing the negative issues etc. Ask them to let you know when they feel complete with it. After they have done this and feel complete, ask them to look into the area and see if the shape is still there. It may be completely gone now, but if it is still there, proceed with more psychic surgery. This time, the shape should release completely. Then do Reiki on the area to fill it with light. Step back doing karate chop and retracting your Reiki fingers as described above.

You may want to follow psychic surgery with a complete Reiki treatment. One session is often all that is needed to completely heal an issue. However, some issues have more than one level, so a person may get some relief, but then experience more symptoms later as a deeper level of the issue comes up to be healed, If this is the case, simply do more psychic surgery to heal the next level.

It is also important to know that as healing takes place, the person could feel other symptoms such as weakness, headaches, diarrhea etc. as the body adjusts to the healing process and begins cleansing. This is sometimes called a healing crisis and is part of the healing.

To minimize this, it is important that the client drink more water, eat lightly and eat more cleansing foods, get more rest and possibly use cleansing herbs, and do other things that facilitate inner cleansing.

This technique works. It is powerful and is easily learned by anyone willing to take the time to try it. All of our problems are within our ability to solve and it is important to realize that there is always a higher purpose for everything in our lives. What we consider to be a problem may actually be an opportunity to learn and grow. Using inner guidance and developing new techniques which allow us to tap more deeply into our innate healing abilities is an important part of our growth process as spiritual healers. As we continue toward the end of the millennium, there will be many opportunities to heal deeply and strengthen our connection to our true nature. Let us rejoice in the love and wisdom of life.

Sincerely,

William Lee Rand

TRADITIONAL JAPANESE REIKI

Volume IV.
The Teacher Manual

Traditional Japanese Reiki **Fourth Degree Workshop**

Teacher's Checklist

THE MASTER/TEACHER TRAINING

At the beginning of the workshop
[ ] Welcome, hugs and hellos!
[ ] Registration, names (for certificates) address & telephone numbers
[ ] Explain routine/starting time/intermission/lunch/et.
[ ] Explain your goal as a teacher
[ ] Ask attendees to introduce themselves to the group

Day One
Day Two
and morning and early afternoon of
Day Three
[ ] Reasons to have consistency in the teaching
[ ] The "Cult" syndrome
[ ] Purpose and mechanism of attunements
[ ] Practice of attunements for each level
[ ] Commitment of teacher to students
[ ] General information on
[ ] Energy work
[ ] Reiki associations
[ ] Accessibility to information and supplies
[ ] Anything you feel is important to share

Day Three(evening)
Day Four
[ ] Assist First Degree Reiki Workshop

Day Five
[ ] Assist Second Degree Reiki Workshop

Day six
[ ] Assist Third Degree Reiki Workshop
[ ] **Distribute certificates**
[ ] Closing (with Third Degree class).

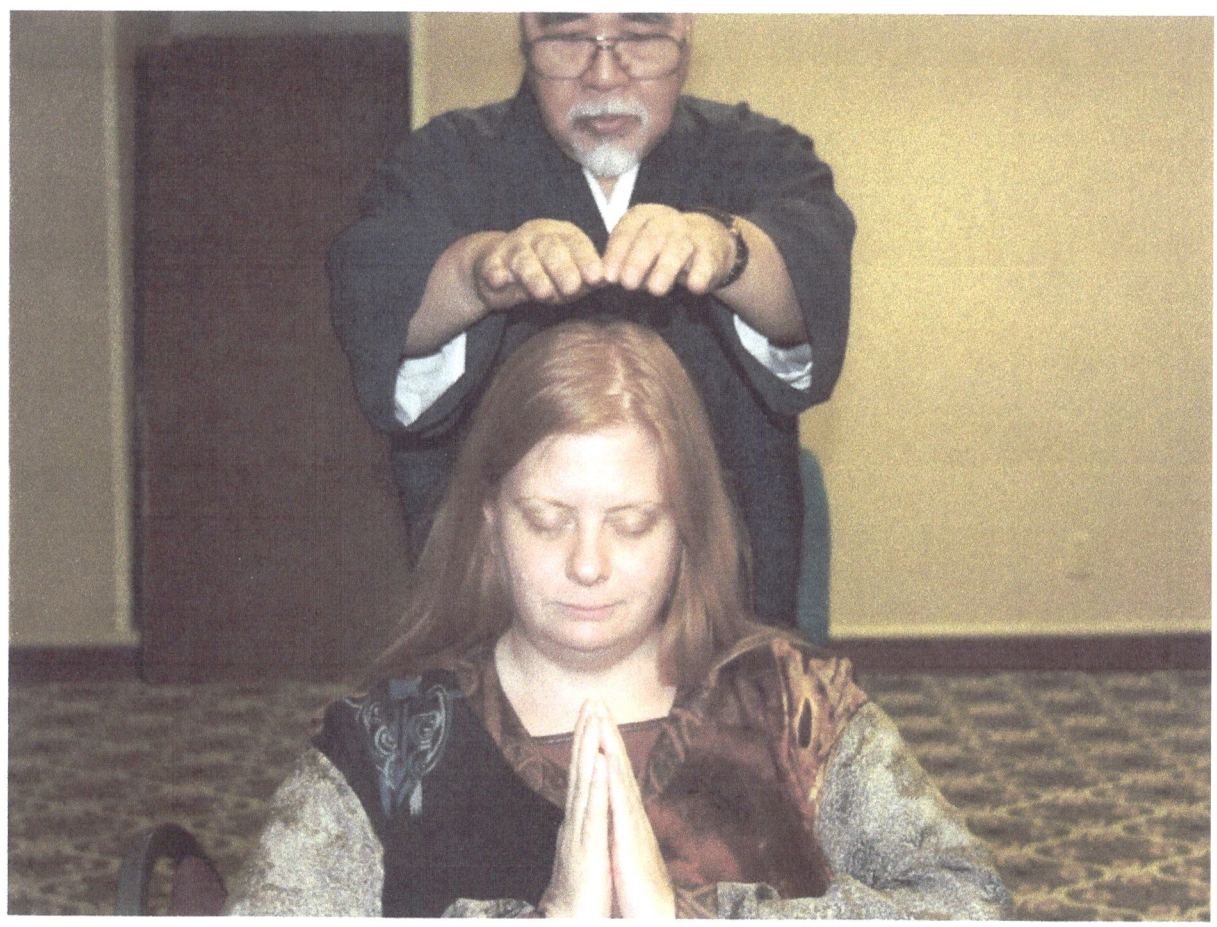

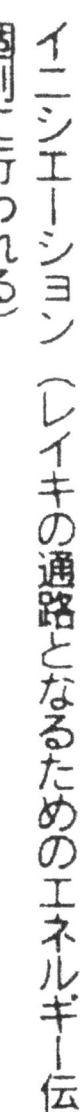

THE HEALING ATTUNEMENT

Perform procedure

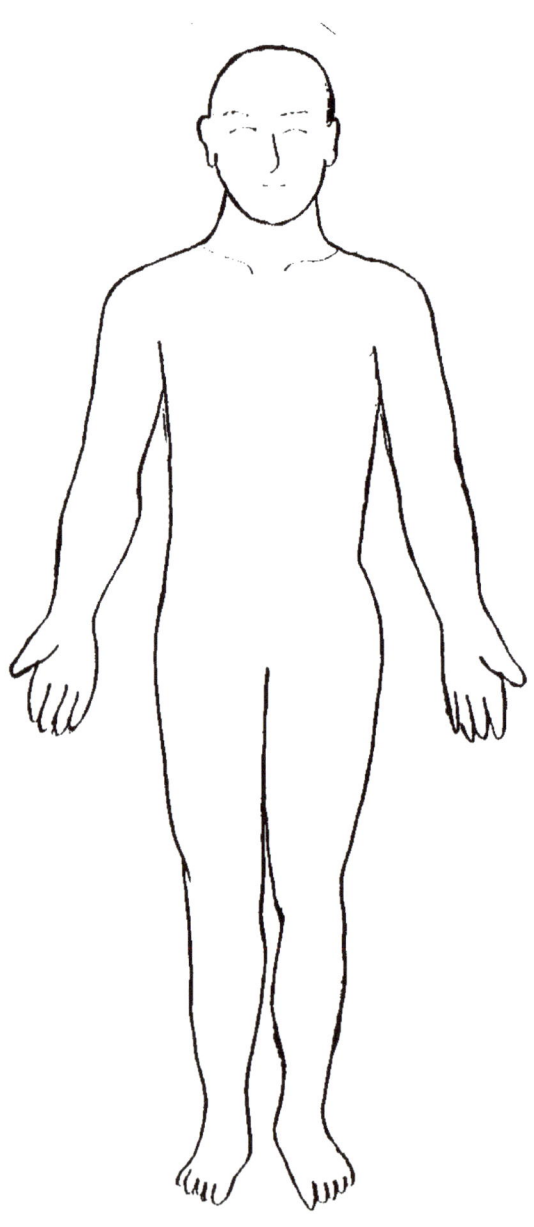

THE HEALING ATTUNEMENT

Perform procedure

Please note:

The Healing Attunement described below is the result methods learned taking courses from different Reiki Master/Teachers and an inspiration during an unique Reiki session with a client.

THE HEALING ATTUNEMENT

There will be situations when you feel your client requires more than a regular Reiki session. The Healing Attunement is very effective at removing energies that blocks the client at having what they consciously want.

The intent is to attune the client to their own vision

- Ask your client to see themselves *(completely healed)* in a real-life situation.

- Keep their eyes closed, hold that vision and smile at it, role play that vision in their mind's eye and keep their hands in the prayer position during the complete attunement.

- Standing behind the client, draw the **Dai Ko Mio** in front of you and move it over your body.

- Draw the **Sei Heki** over the client's head and drape your client with it.

- *BOW* to acknowledge their presence, as to say "Hello" or "I see you"

- Clear the client's energy by making 3 descending sweeps of the hands from above your client's head to the floor.

- Place your right hand on top of your client's head, and your left hand just above your right hand. Hold and **perform procedure.**

- Place your hands on client's shoulders. Hold and **perform procedure.**

- Move to the left side of client: Left arm folded, elbow against your body, raise and turn up your left hand to connect with the Universal Energy. Place your right hand on client's occiput. Hold and **perform procedure until bored.**

- <u>Sit or kneel in front of client</u> and place your hand on client's ankles. Hold just below the ankle bone and **perform procedure.**

- <u>Stand in front of your client</u> and place your hands over their hands held in prayer.

- Hold and **perform procedure.**

- Open/separate your client's hands.

- Place your hands slightly above your client's hand. Hold that position and **perform procedure.**

- Place your hands slightly under your client's hands. Hold that position and **perform procedure.**

- Place one hand slightly above your client's right hand and your other hand slightly under your client's hand. Hold that position and **perform procedure.**

- Place one hand slightly above your client's left hand and your other hand slightly under your client's hand. Hold that position and **perform procedure.**

- <u>Stand in front of client</u> and place the client's hand back into the prayer position and blow continuously along the space between the hands going from the thumb side palm, to the little finger side palm with the intention of sealing their vision into their hands. Rotate the client's hand while doing so.

- Still holding the client's hands, give a short, sharp blast of breath to the client's Crown Chakra, Heart Chakra and Dantien Chakra (just below the navel).

- <u>Move back to the left side of client</u> and again:

    Left arm folded, elbow against your body, raise and turn up your left hand to connect with the Universal Energy. Place your right hand on client's occiput and **perform procedure until bored.**

- <u>Standing behind the client</u> draw the **Sei** Heki over the client's head and drape your client with it.

- Clear the client's energy by making 1 ascending sweeps of the hands from the floor to above your client's head. "Zip them up", so to speak

- <u>BOW</u> to signal the end of your participation, as if saying "Good Bye"

- Your client's hand still in the prayer position:

- Take client's right hand and place it on client's left shoulder. Take client's left hand and place it on client's right shoulder.

- Place your hands on client's shoulders and give your client a gentle tug, and say:

    "Take a slow deep breath, open your eyes, and stretch.

TEACHING INFORMATION

The following can be purchased on Amazon:

- Reiki Pure and Simple Volume I: The Sacred Rites
- Reiki Pure and Simple Volume II: The Most Important Methods of Reiki
- Reiki Pure and Simple Volume IV: The Teacher Manual

** Delivery varies between 2 and 4 weeks depending on your location.

At present, I will continue to supply you with certificates for Reiki:

- Level I, Level II and Level III
- These certificates include a place to sign with your name and your RTC certification number.
- You will design and supply your own Master/Teacher certificate.

As you know, you may contact me anytime by calling me 24/7 at

780.448.0817 (Land Line)

As well as by e-mail at anny@success-and-more.com

With Love and Light,
Sincerely,

Anny

MEDITATION ON THE SYMBOLS.

Have an appropriate music playing and turn the music down when srarting recording the meditation, and make sure it is safe for you to close your eyes when listening this recording.

Greetings!

Please make yourself as comfortable as possible, loosening anything that binds you in anyway.

Now that you are comfortable, listen very closely to my voice and follow suggestions and you will come back to full awareness, feeling refreshed, relaxed, renewed, rejuvenated at peace with yourself and with the world around you.
As you are contemplating what you have learned about Reiki, close your eyes.

Contemplate what you have learned. Especially the symbols and realize that those symbols are attuned to focus and to clarify your intent. Symbols are in fact affirmations written in another language.

There are four Usui Reiki affirmations written in what we call symbols.
The number one symbol, Choku Rei is called the power symbol. Originated in a culture pre-dated Tibetan, the symbol is about forty thousand years old and the Meiji Emperor of Japan used it to assert his commands.

Then there is a second, the number two symbol, the Sei Heki which is the harmony symbol. With self-acceptance and self-love comes peace of mind. A derivative from Sanskrit, it can be written in two ways, one is Japanese, one is Indict.

Then the number three, the distance symbol.
This symbol can be broken down in five Kanji characters.
HON, for book, source, origin.
SHA for person,
ZE, for right, just.
SHO for correct, and
NEN for thought, idea, wish.

The sentence means connect to the right idea, event, or person. It is common practice in esoteric Buddhism to add up several Kanji characters and then scramble them.

Then the number four, the master symbol, the master key that opens all doors is also written in Kanji.

So take a slow deep breath and as you exhale, contemplate the symbols and what message they convey. And as you are contemplating this, you will find yourself on a path, a pathway leading to a fence and there is a gate in that fence. As you are walking there pondering about what you have learned you reach the gate.
In your mind, put your hand on the gate and pause for a moment. You can see the pathway going further.

So, open the gate, pass through the gate, close the gate behind you and you walk on the pathway as a sense of anticipation is starting to flow all over you. You are about to experience the symbols as they are called in a very special and rich way.

As you are walking on the pathway, you are encountering a mist. It is quite light in the beginning and as you are walking on the pathway, it is getting denser and denser. Quite dense and you feel safe. You can still see where you are walking.

You know you are about to experience the symbols and now the mist is getting lighter and in front of you, suspended in the mist is the Choku Rei. Notice the power symbol, the Choku Rei. Notice the spiral. How it gathers all the energy towards it's centre. Attuned to focus. There is a lot of power in the focus. It is there suspended in front of you in the mist. Notice the colour. Does it have a sound? Pass through it as it is suspended in the mist so that you can have a sense of it from the core of your being.

Choku Rei, Choku Rei, Choku Rei. As you are gathering the energy to the eye of the spiral, you commend your universe, commanding the way in that particle point. Enjoy the Choku Rei, enjoy the Choku Rei.

And as you take a slow deep breath and exhale, you notice that the Choku Rei is fading away, as the number two symbol, the harmony symbol is starting to appear. The harmony symbol. Notice how its form expresses balance and harmony. It expresses the freedom that comes with balance and harmony. Perfect balance within the whole system.

Sei Heki, Sei Heki, Sei Reki - balance, a balance of the body and a balance of the mind. Notice how gracious it is as it is moving about. Notice how it feels when it comes above your head. Balance and harmony. Balance and harmony. Notice the colour. Notice the sounds. Notice the feel of it and as you take a slow deep breath and exhale, notice how it graciously fades away and here comes the number three symbol. The distance symbol.

Hon Sha Ze Sho Nen. Hon Sha Ze Sho Nen. Hon Sha Ze Sho Nen. My energy sees your energy. The Buddha in me sees the Buddha in you. Notice the Hon Sha Ze Sho Nen. This symbol helps you make the right connection. It is the symbol who calls forth a person or an event. It is like a bridge. Notice how it can elongate itself in five very precise forms or as the bridge is building, it condenses itself into one piece so to speak.

Hon Sha Ze Sho Nen. It is connecting your psyche to the right person or to the right event and bringing it into your presence. Into the now.

Notice how it can move just like a bridge. It can be straight. It can be slightly curved on the left or on the right. It can have the very beautiful curve of a bridge that goes slightly up and down again. It can bridge yourself to the future. Notice the curves. It can bridge yourself to the past. Or it can curve to the left, curve to the right or go straight in front of you. Notice how the paths of the Hon Sha Ze Sho Nen can move and enjoy the experience.

Notice its colour. Does it make a sound? Truly, enjoy the experience.
And as it is gently fading away, after a gracious bow, here comes number four symbol.

The master symbol. Notice its colour. Does it make a sound? Notice it's form. Notice the three components. It shows a man with arms and legs spread wide. It shows a torch carried by a man and one leg of the man also shows the strength of that man as that man is carrying a light. And then the sun and the moon. The two sides of everything. The two sides of everything. Experience the Dai Ko Myo. Go through it, as it is suspended in front of you, shimmering in the light Find the core of it.

Experience the vibes so to speak of the Dai Ko Myo and realize that it states "I am carrying my light".

As you are carrying your light, realize you are a light and as you are becoming aware of your own light, realize your energy. You are energy. So enjoy the Dai Ko Myo. Let it flow through you. Allow it to remind you of who you are within yourself Enjoy it and as you are gently smiling as to the realization of what this symbol is reminding you of, it is gently bowing and as it is disappearing so to speak, here comes the Hon Sha Ze Sho Nen, the gracious Sei Heki and then the Choku Rei.

And now with an understanding at a deeper level of what the whole thing is all about, a tool to focus, a tool to help you to be very clear of your intents. In your mind, turn around, walk back through the dense mist. Then, the mist is getting much lighter.

You can see the fence and the gate. Pause for a moment as you are having a hand on the gate. Open the gate, pass through the gate, close the gate behind you and gently come back to the room.

Gently come back to now, feeling refreshed, relaxed, renewed, rejuvenated, at peace with yourself and with the world around you.

Anny Slegten
The Reiki Training Centre of Canada.

And what is your fee?

By Anny Slegten, Certified Clinical Hypnotherapist
An article published in the February 2006 issue of Mosaic Magazine.

How much do you charge? What is your fee?

How many times have you asked that question? How many times have you been asked that question?

As a person that is self employed or running your own business, how do you feel when asked that question? What goes through your mind and how do you respond?

It is true that one must be reasonable - both the person who charges and the person who is paying for the services. You need to consider your training, time, money and the energy you've invested in your pursued occupation. How good are you at what you are doing? Is it your passion? How much do you value what you are doing?

A spouse sent her husband (a shop owner) over to me for a hypnotherapy session. She wanted to discover why it was that they never had enough money. Although work was abundant, he had lots of clients and good employees, his business didn't generate enough money to even support his own family. During the hypnotherapy session, he revealed that many customers would drop in at his shop unannounced with a small job that would only take him five minutes to fix. He explained he did not feel justified to charge for something so simple. By making him aware of the total time taken each day by 'small-job-drop-ins', he realized his productivity was down 50% … and so was his income.

I asked him to consider the number of years he spent in trade school and then to add in the number of years he was an apprentice and a journeyman. The total, I recall, was 17 years. When I asked him how well and how fast he thought that 'a small job' would be done by an unskilled tradesman, my client was speechless. Deepening his trance, I then suggested that, in reality, the 'five-minute jobs' were actually the results of 17 years of experience + five minutes of expertise and charging an appropriate and reasonable fee for services rendered was justified. This shift in the worth of his expertise changed his life.

I experienced this for myself recently. I called a service man to repair my overhead garage door which would not open properly and made worrisome noises as I struggled to have it close. The repair man pushed the open/close button a few times, went to his van and came back with a step ladder, a hammer and a screwdriver. He went up the stepladder, unscrewed something, gave one rail a good blow with the hammer, screwed the thing back on, got down the stepladder and it was done! It took him about 15 minutes total and then he handed me the bill. The charge was for one hour.

As I was happily writing him a cheque for the amount requested, the service man (genuinely puzzled by my behavior) mentioned that I looked happy. Of course I was, I said! He had been working for the company during the summer vacations for four years, went to NAIT for apprenticeship in that field for two years (if my memory serves me well) and was working full time as a tradesman for three years now. I explained that, had he not known what he was doing, the repair could have cost me much more than the one hour he charged. In my view, I was paying that amount for $4 + 2 + 3 = 9$ years and 15 minutes. I truly believe I had received great value for the money I paid.

Our hidden ideas about self worth and the worth of certain skills lead me to explore and then incorporate some important questions/training with my hypnotherapy students. During their training as hypnotherapists, I lead my students into a hypnotized regression where I say: "Allow your mind to slide back to something that impressed your mind on how a healer should be paid …" Their answers inevitably reveal how well they are going to do for themselves as Hypnotherapists – not based on how good they are at it but solely based on the type of past beliefs they have! However, I then follow this up with a journey back within to address their beliefs in a way that will be more beneficial to them.

It is also very important to investigate what you think about your field of occupation. What is your belief about what a person should be paid in your field of occupation? Deep down inside, do you respect that field of occupation? How do you expect to do well and to be successful? How do you expect to be paid? The answers to these questions will ultimately always reveal why someone is not making a good living in the field of their choice.

Other valid questions to ask yourself are: "What are my beliefs regarding money and where do these beliefs come from"? If your belief is "money is the root of all evil" then you are never going to have an abundance of money (if you consider yourself to be a 'good' person)! Exploring (and dispelling) your beliefs about just this one area can change your life!

Also, do you need something that will do or do you want something that will last - that has both quality and quantity?

There was a 'special buy' sale on six-volt batteries. We needed one, so we bought two at that price. As usual, my husband wrote the date put into service on top of the 'radar light' battery. It went dead very quickly compared to the ones we usually buy. How come? The dismantled six volt 'radar light'" batteries revealed 16 batteries in the regular one compared to only 12 batteries in the 'special buy' one.

This reminds me of a regular hypnotherapy client that came to me over a period of a few years, driving about 3 hours one way for her hypnotherapy session Then, for a stretch of time, I did not see her.

When she came back to me she said: "Anny, a new hypnotherapist came to my town and I did not have to drive that far to see her. She also cost less. So I changed over to her. But after two years of therapy, I have not seen any progress with myself or my issues. I should have stayed with you: You may cost more but you equally benefit me much more".

So when you ask 'how much?' is your focus on cost or is your focus on value?

The choice is yours. So is the outcome.

Anny is a Clinical Hypnotherapist in private practice since 1984. For information on the services and training she offers in this fascinating field, visit www.success-and-more.com

TRADITIONAL JAPANESE REIKI

General Information

Reiki Release and Consent Form

I, the undersigned, acknowledge and recognize that Reiki is a natural "hands-on" method of energy balancing. The hand positions pictured below have been fully explained to me. It is my responsibility, as the client, to let the Reiki Practitioner know, before the session, if I am uncomfortable with any of the hand positions that are illustrated in the diagrams below and that the Reiki Practitioner and myself will remain fully clothed for the session.

I understand that those under the age of consent require their parent or guardian to attend all sessions. I understand that all services given to me are not offered as a substitute for, or a replacement of, any treatments or therapies for physical, mental, or emotional ailments.

I further understand that the Reiki Practitioner is not a physician and dos not practice psychotherapy, and that payment of fees for services rendered is an acknowledgment of my entire satisfaction with the services provided.

Reiki Hand Positions

Head

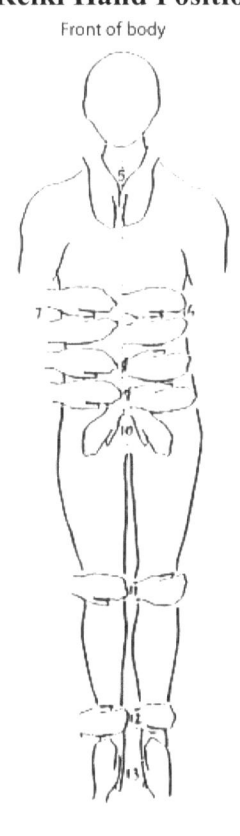

Front of body

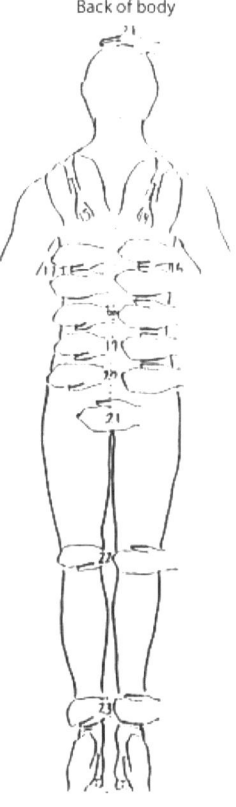

Back of body

Name (please print): _____

Address: _____

City/Town: _____ Telephone: Home _____

Province: _____ Work _____

Postal Code: _____ Occupation: _____

Date of birth: _____ Today's Date: (D/M/Y) _____

Signature of Client/Parent/Guardian: _____

Reiki Training Centre of Canada   Anny Slegten, P.O. Box 3294, Sherwood Park, Alberta, Canada T8H 2T2
Telephone 780.448.0817 Toll Free 1.800.330.5999 Facsimile 780.922.1147 www.reiki-canada.com

THE JAPANESE WRITING ON THE REIKI CERTIFICATE, WHAT DOES IT MEAN?

Japanese writing has up to seven levels of understanding.

意霊気を昂然として

和霊気をつくる

Awaken,

stir up,

energize

the Energy of the Spirit,

the Universal Life Energy (Reiki),

and harmonize,

become one,

be in synchronization

with the Energy of the Spirit,

the Universal Life Energy (Reiki).

Love & light,

Anny

Anny Slegten
Reiki Master/Teacher

Reiki

From an article published in *Feel Good Alberta*, March / April 1996
By Anny Slegten
Master/Teacher of Traditional Japanese Reiki

Reiki.
Pronounced "ray – kee".
Just the sound of the name evokes exotic places, and when we see the Kanji characters it confirms what we suspected: This is "something" from the orient. Ah! Japan, China, Tibet, lands of myths and magic, faraway places so different to what we are accustomed to. For the ones who wonder what Reiki is all about, Reiki is a household word in Japan. It usually signifies energy, depending on the context.

What is it? The Usui Method of Natural Healing known to us as Reiki was rediscovered in Japan in the late 1800's by Mikao Usui (1865-1926), a Buddhist monk. Believing energy work takes a lifetime to master and seeking for a better way to enlightenment, at about 40 years of age Mikao Usui went to the top of a mountain. At the time, it was normal for a Buddhist Monk to sit on a mountain to meditate. Some also were going there to die. According to the legend, Mikao Usui sat there for 21 days, an unusually long time, and had a vision, a realization he promptly shared first with other fellow monks, and then with others outside the monastery.

What Mikao Usui gave us is a most beautiful and powerful way to experience the flow of the Universal Life Force Energy through our entire being and we usually first feel it in the palm of our hands. To my knowledge, it is the easiest, organized way to teach energy work. Clarifying the intent with symbols, Reiki teaches us the power of focusing. Our focus gives direction to the energy, our intent gives it the job. Therefore, once we have learned to awaken the Universal Life Force Energy and then be in tune with it, we can effectively help ourselves and others physically and emotionally in many ways. The laying on of hands is one of them. Following our focus and our intent, Reiki travels through time and space. Reiki goes through walls, clothing, leather, jewelry. A session an be given anywhere. When in tune with it, Reiki gives the practitioner and the receiver a profound understanding of what life is all about.

Because Reiki responds to our focus and our intent, it is interesting to observe what is happening within the Reiki community itself. There are some fantastic stories on how the rediscovery of Reiki came about. Stories passed on orally have a tendency of becoming exaggerated, and so are the rituals, and Reiki has followed the same path. How do I know? Well, I have connections in high places, you know, and in Japan too. In my search for the origin of the Usui System of Natural Healing I experienced and observed Reiki classes with over ten Reiki Master/Teachers.

Some lay it on really thick for their students, not giving people credit for their intelligence. However, the overwhelming majority of Reiki Master/Teachers are sincere and come from the heart. Felling inspired, some Reiki practitioner and teachers change the Sanskrit and the Kanji calligraphy we call symbols. Some are so distorted one wonders where this all came from. The same goes for the way some Reiki classes are conducted: exotic and enchanting, much more Japanese than in Japan.

So when something about the Reiki class is not sitting well with you, remember to separate the message from the messenger. Check things out, the information, the teacher. Go to the source. I called the Reiki Masters of the Reiki Teachers, verified my Reiki Teacher's claims and credentials, asked where the information that was being taught came from, and pursued, and pursued. This was quite an eye opener.

The Truth of the matter is no symbols are more powerful than others. It is your focus and your intent that makes the symbol. Reiki is not about money, it is not about who is better than whom, it is not about who has the most powerful symbols. Reiki is so powerful, the system works no matter how you paint it. Because it is pure energy, it follows the practitioners focus and thoughts and easily transfers agendas from one person to another. Reiki is about the Life Force Energy, the Collective Intelligence that flows through our very own being. When practiced and taught as Mikao Usui intended, Reiki is about coming home to the realization that a wonderful empowering healing energy is available to all who desire and seek. Reiki is about being in tune with life itself.

The beauty of the Usui System of Natural Healing we call Reiki lies in its simplicity, let us keep it that way.

By Anny Slegten, Master/Teacher of Traditional Japanese Reiki

This ad included in the magazine article contained an early version of the Reiki Training Centre of Canada logo

Online Store, Contact, and More…

You may contact Anny by visiting any of her websites and scroll down the home page to the contact information.

http://www.annyslegten.com
    Anny's private website and online store.

http://www.success-and-more.com
    To find the description of the many services offered, and more.

http://www.htialberta.com
    The Hypnotism Training Institute of Alberta including descriptions of hypnosis and hypnotherapy courses given.

http://www.reiki-canada.com
    About the Reiki Training Centre of Canada.

http://www.slegtenianhypnosis.com
    Although open to anyone interested in this fascinating hypnosis modality, this website information is for graduates of the Hypnotism Training Institute of Alberta.

http://www.connectwithanny.com
    This is the best place to keep up to date with Anny – including seeing all her latest books and how to order them on Amazon.

Other books by Anny Slegten

This book is a must read for Reiki Practitioners
regardless of their spiritual lineage
and could be of great benefit to Energy Healers
http://www.reiki-canada.com

The Many Ways of Reiki
http://www.reiki-canada.com

The Reiki Training Centre of Canada
Teacher's Manual
http://www.reiki-canada.com

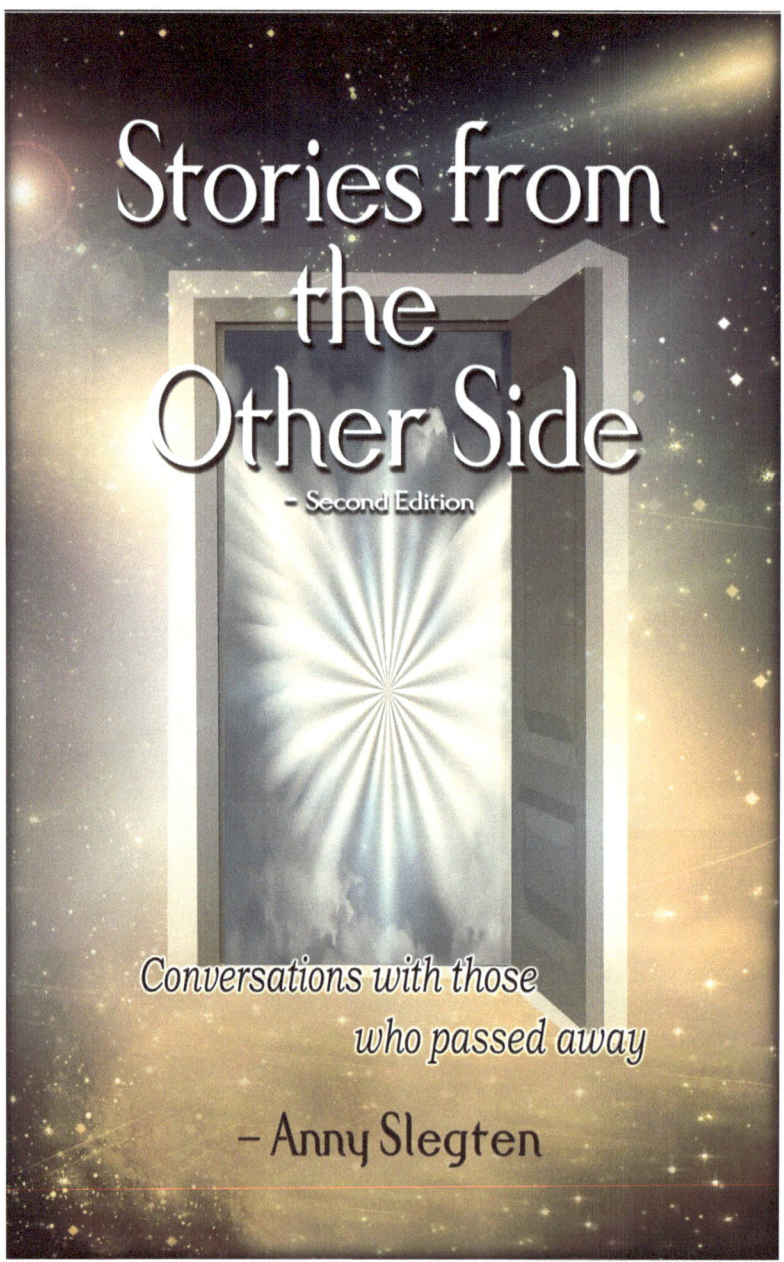

Stories from The Other Side – Second Edition
http://www.connectwithanny.com

The Four Mental Agreements
To Losing Weight
http://www.connectwithanny.com

TRADITIONAL JAPANESE REIKI
Your Personal Notes

YOUR NOTES:

YOUR NOTES:

YOUR NOTES:

YOUR NOTES:

YOUR NOTES:

YOUR NOTES:

YOUR NOTES:

YOUR NOTES:

Who is Anny Slegten?

A Reiki Master, Anny teaches the four levels of the "Usui Method of Natural Healing". This is known by the name of "Usui Reiki" as it presently is taught in Japan. It is also called "Traditional Japanese Reiki" as well as "Reiki" as practiced in North America.

Anny was formally introduced to Life Force Energy training in North Bay, Ontario, Canada, in 1976, and was initiated into Reiki in Alberta in March 1992.

Anny is grateful to all the Reiki Masters who helped her in her search for the source of the Usui System of Natural Healing known to us as Reiki.

Anny was initiated as a Reiki Master/Teacher in 1995. In 1996 she was initiated as a Tibetan Reiki Master/Teacher and took her Karuna™ Reiki Master/Teacher Training in February 1997.

In September 1999 Anny attended the Japanese Reiki Techniques Training maned "The Most Important Methods for Reiki" with Frank Arjava Petter – a Reiki Master/Teacher who lived in Japan for about 12 years and is the author of many excellent books on Reiki.

In May 2006 Anny completed Komyo Reiki Shinpiden by Reverend Hyakuten Inamoto, who is an accredited Shihan/Teacher of the Koato Reiki Kai (Kyoto Center), Japan.

Anny's Belgian parents were from the Flemish part of Belgium and were speaking Flemish (Dutch) at home. Living in Congo, everything was in French.

Although she never spoke Flemish (Dutch), Anny speaks English with a guttural Dutch/German accent. Living in the English-speaking part of Canada for decades, Anny now speaks French with an English accent!

As Director of The Hypnotism Training Institute of Alberta and The Reiki Training Centre of Canada, Anny has developed and structured the training and curriculum to the highest standards for both The Hypnotism Training Institute of Alberta and the Reiki Training Centre of Canada. She offers training to students that come from all over Canada and around the world.

Anny is an Author and holds certifications as:

- *Reiki Master/Teacher*
- *Master Remote Viewer*
- *Master Hypnotist*
- *Clinical Hypnotherapist*
- *Hypno-Baby Birthing Facilitator and Instructor*
- *HypnoBirthing™ Fertility Therapist for Men & Women*

Anny is a world renowned Clinical Hypnotherapist
Hypnologist in full time practice since 1984 as well as a Hypno-Energy worker since 2008.

1986 Anny created and developed an unique method using hypnosis for distance services.

Over the years these Virtual Sessions proved to be an useful, effective and efficient method for investigations, resolution and putting closure on both present and past issues. This would assist such events as clearing land, places, buildings, healing people (alive or dead) in need of help.

To know more about Anny, please visit www.annyslegten.com and make sure to read what she published on her Blog.

Do you wonder what else Anny is publishing?
Visit http://www.connectwithanny.com

www.ingramcontent.com/pod-product-compliance
Lightning Source LLC
Chambersburg PA
CBHW040904020526

44114CB00037B/51